How to be a Business Partner by Performance Consulting

Nigel Harrison

performance consulting : uk

How to be a True Business Partner by Performance Consulting

by Nigel Harrison

Published by Nigel Harrison

32 Victoria Road
Sheffield
S10 2DL

ISBN: 978-0-9559068-0-0

Layout and graphics by Jonathan Horner [email@jonhorner.co.uk]

Proof editing by Annette Waterhouse [annette.waterhouse@bigfoot.com]

Typeset, printed and bound by CPI Anthony Rowe, Chippenham.

Cover photograph by Elsie Harrison from her first ascent of Kesevan in Kyrgyzstan.

Contents

This book is aimed at people who are:

- business partners or in any other internal consulting role.
- It will be especially valuable to people who have:
    - read Improving Employee Performance by Nigel Harrison published by Kogan Page, which introduces a 7-step Performance Consulting process.
    - attended my three day Performance Consulting Skills workshop (called "Quantifying Performance Gaps" in AstraZeneca and "Solving Performance Problems" in LloydsTSB).

Acknowledgements

With thanks to Steve Hill and Morven Smith for their valuable additions to the first draft; to Allan Watkinson and Phil Dickinson for their comments on the second draft; and to all the attendees on the Reuters and Xerox Master Classes for their ideas and feedback.

In addition, my thanks to my daughter Elsie for her photographs from her first ascent in Kyrgyzstan.

Nigel Harrison 2008

About the author

Nigel Harrison is a chartered Business Psychologist and founder of Performance Consulting UK Ltd.

He has worked in the industry for 25 years, helping organisations to set up internal consulting groups. During this time he developed a three day skills workshop on Performance Consulting Skills.

The process is used by internal consultants in AstraZeneca, Reuters IS, Lloyds TSB, Scottish Widows, Abbey, Nationwide, Giro Bank, AXA, AMP, Norwich Union and Xerox.

In 2000 Kogan Page asked Nigel to write a book on called Improving Employee Performance based on the 7-step problem analysis process used in the three day workshop.

In recent years Nigel has been coaching consultants to be more effective in organisations and has developed an advanced skills workshop, which includes a follow-up day when he reviews the successes and setbacks that people have experienced in applying a consulting process to their organisations.

The ideas and opinions in this book are based on the real experiences of hundreds of internal consultants in a variety of organisations. It is not a theoretical or rigorous study. The content is meant to be challenging and opinionated, to try to get close to the reality that many internal consultants experience.

What is written here is not "true". You need to relate these ideas to your own experience, decide what works for you, try the ideas out in reality and determine what is "true" for you. Good luck!

Nigel Harrison

1

What does it mean to be a business partner?

Contents

1.1 **What is a business partner?**

A business partner is someone who uses a consulting approach in partnership, to help their clients to face up to their own problems and find appropriate solutions.

When you can do all these things your client will start to respect you as a partner and you will have become a true business partner.

How will I know if I am a "true" business partner?

The sort of things that you will start to see are:

- You are brought in very early to help resolve issues before they become solutions;
- You are entrusted with confidential information;
- Your clients will share their plans with you;
- You become a "confidant";
- Your clients trust you enough to ask for ad-hoc and personal advice;
- You can challenge the client without losing trust.

(With thanks to Steve Hill)

Ulrich's 3-box model

About twenty years ago Ulrich proposed a 3-box model of business partnership, which has been adopted by many organisations.

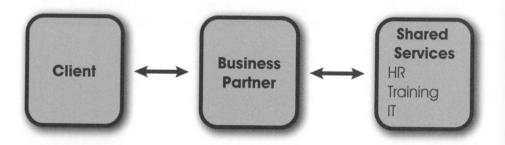

The benefits of this approach were that it allowed centralisation and cost reduction of shared corporate resources whilst the client had a one-stop-shop for internal suppliers.

The job of the business partner is to help analyse the client's needs and their contracts with appropriate suppliers.

When the role works well the business partner is a respected partner of the business, stopping much of the **solutioneering** (clients jumping to solutions) and helping to prioritise a set of realistic requirements for the suppliers.

It works badly when the business partner is merely a letterbox, passing orders on to the suppliers and adding little value. Business partners can sometimes even "go native", giving their loyalty to the client and acting aggressively to win scarce resource before other business areas can get their hands on it. Additionally, a business partner can also become a blockage or gatekeeper to organisational resource and wield power by not authorising solutions.

What sort of business partners do you have in your organisation?

Are the people in the role true business partners?

What about other internal consultants?

In this book I use the term "business partner" in a generic way to cover any internal consulting role. Indeed, as an external consultant you should still be a business partner, and even a sales consultant. The important thing is that you work with your client in partnership at the front-end analysis phase of projects.

1.2 **Why do we need business partners?**

It is very hard to see your own problems clearly, let alone deal with them. The business partner role is like a counsellor or therapist, who helps the client recognise the underlying reasons for patterns of negative behaviour. In counselling it is thought that the client has the solutions within them, if they could only recognise the problem.

The business partner acts in a similar role for the organisation. They act as a mirror for the client in which they can see more clearly their own problems, enabling them to find solutions and put them into action. They also provide access to suppliers such as HR, Training and IT when appropriate.

This book is about the sometimes uncomfortable reality of this "stuck in the middle" role.

Some examples

> **Consultant 1 – The "order taker"**
>
> When the client says "We need a leadership course", the "order taker's" response is:
>
> *"Okay, I know a good one. How many people do you want to go on it? When do you want it done by? We can do it in this year's training budget. I will get it organised."*

Doesn't this business partner sound efficient? But the end result for the organisation is that 40 senior managers attend a "leadership course" at a cost of £200k to the training budget, plus lost opportunity cost; and whilst the participants said they received value, there were no defined business benefits and no measurable value to the organisation. In fact, the course distracted managers from their immediate business priorities. Later in the year the client has to call an emergency meeting to deal with business issues: the business partner is not invited because they are perceived only as "the person who organises courses".

Consultant 2 – The "business partner"

When the client says "We need a leadership course", the "business partner's" response is:

"Okay, who do you want to go on it? What do you want to see them doing when they come back? When have you got some time so we can pin down the business value that you want to see? I just need to ask you a few questions to build the business case – when can you spare some time for that?"

This business partner is still being positive but they are not accepting the "order taker" role. The result is that the business partner ends up working with the client to find out what they actually want (which turns out to be something completely different from what the client originally thought). This approach saves £200k from the training budget and enables the business partner to work on solutions with defined business benefits. Ultimately, the business partner is the first person the client rings when they want to deal with new business issues.

What sort of internal consultant are you? This book is about how to behave as Consultant 2 – as a true business partner.

1.3 **The skills needed to be an effective partner**

The skills needed to become an effective internal consultant and business partner are very similar to the skills needed to be successful in life. You need the ability to:

- Listen;
- Build rapport and trust;
- Think analytically and follow a process;
- Challenge and ask questions to find the causes of problems;
- Be intuitive and creative enough to be able to synthesise solutions;
- Focus on realistic action.

You also need to:

- Silence your own personal needs and demons;
- Be in the here and now;
- Be brave and authentic.

Perhaps the best description of an internal consultant came from Chris Argyris, Professor Emeritus at Harvard Business School, when he said of consultant:

- Has a process;
- Knows where they are in that process;
- Is authentic at all times;
- Acts as a mirror to the client.

Quite a tall order, isn't it?

The good thing about the role is that most people rarely have quality time with someone who can listen and help them think through their own issues.

So even the use of very basic consulting skills and processes will often have very powerful results. So don't worry about being the perfect consultant – you can add real value with fairly simple interventions.

1.4 **The first issue we have to deal with**

Is that our clients **do not** come to us and say: "Please help me with my problem." Instead, they tend to approach us with **solutions**, which are actually performance problems, e.g. "I need leadership training for my managers". (This is what I mean by *solutioneering*.)

Depending on your perceived role (e.g. as "Training Consultant", "IT Consultant" or "HR Consultant"), your client may expect you to be the person who will deliver their solution for them; and the first problem we often have to deal with is our client's expectation that we will merely **take orders** for their designed solutions.

You can tell when a client perceives you as an "order taker" because they will give you very little time, eg. "I only have ten minutes, but I just want you to …" (After all, if they only expect to pass on an order to you, it will not take very long!)

One of the first challenges of a new business partner is to move out of this perceived "order taker" role.

Why do our clients treat us as "order takers"?

Most managers have so many issues to tackle that they often cannot see the wood for the trees. There is great appeal in an instant solution for getting one problem off our back, if only for a short time. HR, IT and Training Departments often play the role of "someone to give a problem to", and line managers often try to use business partners in the same way.

It is also human to make sense of patterns, to join up the dots and make a pattern (Gestalt psychology). We are more comfortable with the concrete than the fluid and most clients jump too quickly to the comfort of solutions and action.

> *"The brain is a mechanism which is constantly trying to extract patterns from the data it receives."*
>
> G.R. Taylor, 1979

Organisations have an inherent pressure to **solutioneer**. Line managers often do not have the bandwidth to think through their complex, integrated problems so they jump to simple solutions:

"We need a Leadership course."

"We need a new Customer Relationship Management System."

"I want to do Myers Briggs for this team."

"We need a team build."

They also look around for additional resource to help them:

"We have made training a priority this year, please arrange more for us!"

The danger of this single solution approach is that it is simplistic. The root causes of the performance problems have not been recognised, and whilst the single solutions will distract attention for a short time, they will most likely ultimately fail. I ask my workshop participants to estimate how many of today's problems are caused by yesterday's solutions – the most common answer is **70–80%**! What do you think it is in your organisation?

After many organisations had spent millions of pounds on instant Training, IT and HR solutions that did not work, it became clear that there was a need for someone who would help line managers analyse their business problems – someone who would act as a commissioning agent to appropriate providers of solutions.

1.5 **The irrational organisation**

My previous book, *Improving Employee Performance*, introduces a simple process for understanding any performance problem and shows that by using it you can solve virtually any problem. However, this assumes that you have a willing client who is prepared to face up to, and actually wants to solve, their problems. In many organisations the dominant culture is one of "fantasy" and blame, where quick fix and impression management are the dominant problem solving methods. In this sort of environment a diagnostic approach can be actively resisted. This book is about coping with the irrational parts of organisational culture whilst still being effective as an internal consultant.

It can be a dangerous place to be.

The business partner is stuck in the middle. You can be perceived by your client as an obstacle in their relationship with suppliers (who they used to deal with directly); and by suppliers as an obstacle in their relationship with your client.

A story

A senior line manager had a problem with employee performance. She discussed it with her business partner:

> *"We need to improve sales by 15% over the next six months. I want your help in getting the branches to double the number of leads they pass on to the Financial Advisors – that should do it easily."*

The business partner worked hard with business managers and within four weeks the number of leads had doubled.

One week later the senior manager challenged the business partner:

> *"What sort of rubbish leads are the branches passing on? Our conversion rate has dropped, my sales people are complaining and we are further down on target! I want you to arrange training the branch staff to qualify leads better."*

The instant **solutioneering** had just wasted time and money because the real cause of the sales gap had not been revealed. The result was that the business partner was moved to a less demanding role because it was thought that they no longer had the credibility to challenge and support the business.

1.6 **Diagnostic problem solving versus quick fix**

It is natural to jump to solutions and many organisations have an strong quick fix culture. Much of the business partner role is helping managers to diagnose the causes of their problems using "**diagnostic problem solving**" as the antidote to "**quick fix**" problem solving.

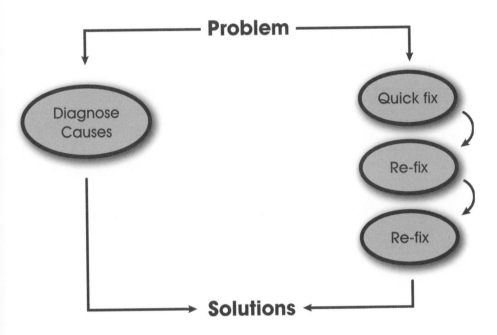

But actually, both of these approaches have their strengths and weaknesses.

As a successful internal consultant you need to work in a diagnostic way but with the speed of the quick fix. We need to harness the strengths of each approach.

Diagnostic problem solving

Strengths	Solutions based on causes so are most likely to work first time.
Weaknesses	Can take time, 'paralysis by analysis'.

Quick fix problem solving

Strengths	Allows instant action and the impression of progress.
Weaknesses	You can waste time and money fixing the wrong thing.

The ideal solution is a fast diagnostic phase followed by immediate action.

1.7 **Fantasy and reality in organisations**

I am sorry to have to break this to you but organisations are not totally rational, honest places! After working for 25 years as a Business Psychologist I have found that only the very best organisations have a level of trust and honesty that allows an "adult" treatment of problems.

Most people are trying to do a good job but often personal self-interest and power can take precedence over what is best for the organisation.

Put into a group where their livelihood depends on their success, most rational people revert to fairly basic defence mechanisms.

Common defence reactions to problems:
- Denial;
- Avoidance (hope it goes away);

- Blame someone else;
- Moan about it;

- Find someone else to give it to;
- Ask an expert;
- Wait for "the man on the white horse" to solve it for us;
- Look in the manual;

- Try a quick fix;
- Pay a supplier to take the problem and responsibility away.

The alternative is:
- Talk to someone you trust about it;
- Face up to it;
- Find the causes and commit to the action needed to solve it.

I am sure you can see that the latter solutions require energy and a level of adult/rational thought. It is often easier to adopt defence mechanisms than to solve the problem.

It is also possible that we may not really want to solve our problems. Often, we think of them as **friends** – we become comfortable with the and, if we lost them, might have to face up to even more uncomfortable truths!

Another reason why problems may not be faced up to is the complexity of organisations and, therefore, of their problems. It is possible that people do not know where the problems are; how many there are; and how they are interlinked.

As internal consultants, we have to be very careful to build the right level of trust and awareness to help clients face up to their own problems.

Part of building this trust with the client is to start to see the world from their point of view. This is why we draw a simple system diagram of the people involved, which usually ends up as a shared "map" of where the problems are.

1.8 **What sort of relationship do our clients really want?**

Clients may have different expectations to you about what sort of relationship they want.

Client's expectation is:

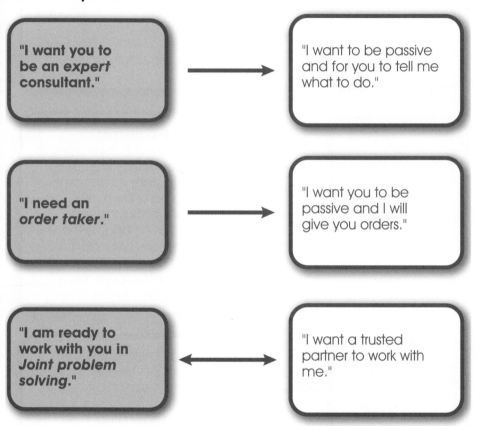

"I want you to be an *expert* consultant." ➡ "I want to be passive and for you to tell me what to do."

"I need an *order taker*." ➡ "I want you to be passive and I will give you orders."

"I am ready to work with you in *Joint problem solving*." ⬅➡ "I want a trusted partner to work with me."

You might be able to categorise your clients into those who want a certain sort of relationship and, therefore, to provide the appropriate type of service.

Client wants: **Consultant's response:**

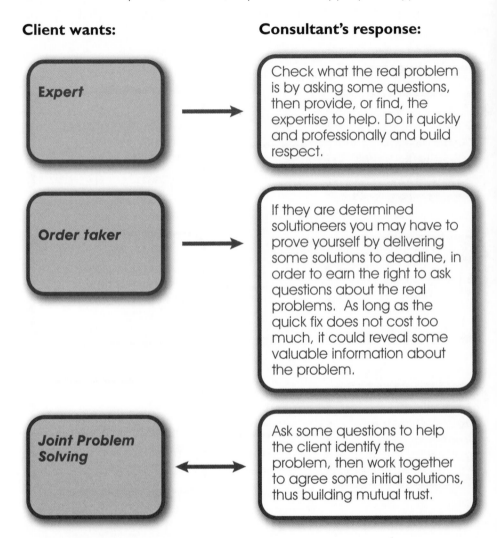

Expert

Check what the real problem is by asking some questions, then provide, or find, the expertise to help. Do it quickly and professionally and build respect.

Order taker

If they are determined solutioneers you may have to prove yourself by delivering some solutions to deadline, in order to earn the right to ask questions about the real problems. As long as the quick fix does not cost too much, it could reveal some valuable information about the problem.

Joint Problem Solving

Ask some questions to help the client identify the problem, then work together to agree some initial solutions, thus building mutual trust.

In all cases you try to move the client towards joint problem solving via a diagnostic approach.

Some examples of client requests

1. The client asks for *expert consulting*:

"What is our policy on external recruitment?"	**Expert reply:** Our policy is…
	Business partner reply: Who are you thinking of? Why is that? If we do not fill it, what will happen? How soon do you need it filled? Have I got a good handle on the problem? Okay, I will look at some options for you.

2. The client wants an *order taker*:

"Can you book my team on a Flash Xtra course?"	**Order taker reply:** Okay, that's on our approved course list – I will get it sorted...
	Business partner reply: Certainly – your whole team? What are they doing with Flash Xtra? What do you want them to be able to do? If they cannot get on this course what will the effect be on your team performance? Have I got a good idea of the problem? Okay, I will look at some options to enable you to achieve what you want.

As a skilled business partner you can respond to requests from your clients in a joint problem solving way and turn their perception of you from an *expert*, or an *order taker*, into someone they trust to work with in joint problem solving.

Clients tend to seek...

The Economic and Social Research Council (ESRC) research on client-consultant relationships found the most important feature clients wanted was a "partnership style" relationship marked by:

- a commitment to, and passion for, the task;
- flexibility;
- a willingness to challenge the client and be challenged;
- openness and integrity;
- the ability to gain the respect of the client's staff;
- an understanding of the client's business.

People Management, 18 May 2006

Forming this style of relationship is one of the key skills of an internal consultant – building enough trust to challenge the client whist at the same time being perceived as helpful, but not allowing the client to avoid their problems. It is a subtle balancing act.

Building rapport and trust

Only when we have built enough rapport and trust by our initial behaviour can we can use the 7-step process as a joint problem-solving process to analyse the cause of any problem.

Summary

First business partner lessons:

- Avoid the "order taker" role;
- Avoid the "expert consultant" role;
- Resist solutioneering;
- Watch out for fantasy and common defence reactions;
- Gain trust and rapport before you get down to the task;
- Behave as a partner;
- Demonstrate openness and integrity;
- Work fast to harness the energy of the quick fix, but use a flexible diagnostic approach to make sure that you are solving the real problem.

The Resilient Consultant

Contents

2.1 **Business partner attributes**

The business partner is stuck in the middle. Your client can perceive you as an obstacle to suppliers (who they used to deal with directly) and by suppliers as an obstacle to their clients!

To prosper in the role I think you need a number of attributes:

Knowledge
- a problem analysis process
- knowledge of potential supplier solutions
- awareness and political ability to map stakeholders

Skills
- networking skills with power holders, clients and suppliers
- listening and questioning (consulting) skills
- high personal credibility with the line and peers
- awareness of self to see it as it is
- personal integrity to say it as it is
- the ability to read others
- the self-awareness to be able to flex your approach

Motivation
- confidence in the purpose of the role
- confidence to resist "solutioneering"
- resilience to overcome setbacks
- perseverance to bring about cultural change

Environment
- support from superiors
- support from colleagues
- access to the people you need

2.2 **Self Assessment Quiz – a brief self-analysis**

On a scale of 0–10 where would you rate yourself now, where would you like to be and what is the cost to you if the gap continues?

Attribute	Rating now	Where I would like to be	The cost of the gap to me if it continues
A problem analysis process	←→		
Knowledge of potential supplier solutions			
Awareness and political ability to map stakeholders			
Networking skills with power holders, clients and suppliers			
Listening and questioning (consulting) skills			
High personal credibility with the line and peers			
Personal integrity to say it as it is			
Awareness of self to see it as it is			
The ability to read others			
The self-awareness and skills to flex your approach			
Confidence in the purpose of your role			
Confidence to resist "solutioneering"			
Resilience to overcome setbacks			
Perseverance to see change through			
Support from superiors			
Support from colleagues			
Access to the people you need			

What is the total cost of the gap if it continues?

What are your priority development areas?

23

Is it worth doing something about it?

How about a little personal development?

From this brief self-analysis, what are your top 3 priority areas for development? Have a look at the next page for some suggestions about what you could do.

```
┌─────────────────────────────────────────────────┐
│ 1                                                 │
│                                                   │
│                                                   │
│                                                   │
│                                                   │
└─────────────────────────────────────────────────┘
┌─────────────────────────────────────────────────┐
│ 2                                                 │
│                                                   │
│                                                   │
│                                                   │
│                                                   │
└─────────────────────────────────────────────────┘
┌─────────────────────────────────────────────────┐
│ 3                                                 │
│                                                   │
│                                                   │
│                                                   │
│                                                   │
└─────────────────────────────────────────────────┘
```

Hopefully this book will help but is not the total solution. Discuss the ideas with your coach. (What, no coach? – I suggest you get one!). The internal consultant role needs skilled performance of a number of sophisticated skills and you need someone to help you reflect, plan to improve and to give you feedback. A personal coach could be very useful.

2.3 **Some suggestions to get you thinking about your development**

Attribute	Some suggested solutions	Ideas for me
A problem analysis process	Use the 7-step process in chapter 3.	
Knowledge of potential supplier solutions	Meet your supplier regularly, find out their expectations of the relationship, attend relevant conferences and read your supplier's journals.	
Awareness and political ability to map stakeholders	Map out your stakeholders, anticipate what their expectations of you are and make a plan to meet them.	
Networking skills with clients and suppliers	Draw a map of your network. Identify people that you do not know – plan to meet them.	
Listening and questioning (consulting) skills	Attend a skills workshop where you can try your skills in a safe environment, receive feedback, reflect, try new things and plan to improve.	
High personal credibility with the line	Read their journals, match their language, draw a map of their business model and environment, take a line job.	
Personal integrity to say it as it is	To be a successful consultant you need to be authentic at all times – make it your mantra.	
Awareness of self to see it as it is	Try some psychological profiles such as Myers Briggs, Emotional Intelligence etc. Search on Google for free on-line tests or go on a workshop.	
The ability to read others	Go on a Myers Briggs workshop, or read *The Art of Speed Reading People* by Tieger and Barron-Tieger or attend a course on NLP.	

Attribute	Some suggested solutions	Ideas for me
The self- awareness and skills to flex your approach	Build a personal development plan to build your awareness, record your successes in flexing your behaviour and learn from them.	
Confidence in the purpose of the role	Meet your boss and clarify the official purpose of the role; then map out all the stakeholders who have an interest in the role and their expectations.	
Confidence to resist "solutioneering"	Work with your coach to develop your skills and successes to build your justified confidence.	
Resilience to overcome setbacks	How good are you at bouncing back? Try the resilience inventory on page 32.	
Perseverance to bring about cultural change	Make a change plan with your boss and arrange regular support, enlist powerful allies early, spend time managing upwards, watch out for ambushes.	
Support from superiors	Meet your boss and be assertive about your needs for support.	
Support from colleagues	Ask them for support. Arrange a "buddy" and a "coach". Attend meetings with a buddy or your coach, review how meetings go, receive feedback, plan to improve next time.	
Access to the people you need	Map out who you need access to, contract clearly with your boss and their bosses and negotiate access.	

Now look at your ideas and put them through this "reality" filter.

Which ideas are you left with?

What are you going to try first?

Add them to your action plan.

Look at your list of possible solutions
Cross out those:
• that are just not feasible;
• whose cost would be greater than the benefit.
Highlight those:
• that can be easily implemented;
• that will give the best results for minimum effort.

Action plan

What	Who?	When?

Set a date to evaluate whether
the performance gap has closed.

_ _ / _ _ / _ _

This is your development plan as a business partner or performance consultant.

2.4 **Building your resilience to overcome setbacks**

What is resilience?

In the same way that people's personalities differ, we also differ in our psychological well-being (general coping skills) and our ability to deal with setbacks.

Whether life events cause us stress depends on how we perceive those events and the amount of support we have available. The ability to cope and deal with stressful events is called resilience.

As an internal consultant you can be stuck in a "piggy-in-the-middle" role where you suffer unreasonable stress. The ability to cope with this and bounce back to do the right thing is a key characteristic of success.

Building competence is the main way of increasing one's psychological resilience.

Examples of Internal Consultant stress

As a business partner (of any type) you will often suffer from unrealistic pressure and blame:

Example 1

Pressure on the learning and development manager from his director, because the main client groups have been complaining at board level that his team was not delivering enough relevant training. At the same time the CEO has cut training spend by 20%.

(In fact available training had increased: line managers were not sending people due to lack of time, and senior managers had chosen "more training" as their main solution to achieving their performance targets without consulting the training department.)

Example 2

Pressure from the CEO to the HR director about the fact that the recruitment process could take 6 months. This was perceived as too long, meaning their managers were complaining that they could not reach their targets because of a lack of staff, and that this was HR's fault.

(In fact the HR part of the recruitment process was only 8 weeks and was delivered on time; the remaining delays were down to management inefficiency and the root cause was poor leadership, leading to high turnover of staff.)

Example 3

An IT department was blamed for a costly project failure. The new IT director is told by the board that the next one must not fail, but actually the same project is re-started with a new name and new deadlines, but with no time for re-analysis of the problem. The IT relationship manager is told to make sure it is delivered on time this time.

(In fact the project failed because the solution was too big and unwieldy and was not linked to an analysis of the causes of problem.)

With all these problems the business partner or relationship manager starts with:

- unrealistic expectations of the role;
- pressure to perform;
- strong messages to get on with delivery;
- messages from the clients that they do not want challenge;
- emotional investment in a dominant fantasy.

These take emotional courage to resist and emotional resilience to keep going, despite setbacks and pressure not to analyse the cause of problems.

Business partners can suffer:

- blame;
- pressure;
- psychological games;
- a lack of support.

All of which can lead to high levels of stress.

One of the biggest stresses in life stressors ambiguity and lack of power over your own destiny – which is where the business partner can find him- or herself!

How do we stay resilient to pressure

Each person is different but we can learn from the work done on resilience. (Most of what follows comes from the work of Reivich and Shatte in The Resilience Factor, which I recommend.) We all react differently to setbacks or adversity:

Adversity is an event that stimulates a reaction from us.

Beliefs are our thoughts, which govern how we respond to adversity.

Consequences are the emotional and behavioural results of **A**+**B**.

We are not in control of **A** but we can influence how we react to **B** and the **C**onsequences.

People who are resilient tend to have realistic optimism – a positive outlook without denying reality.

They also have "accurate thinking" – a firm grasp of reality.

They can recognise their ABCs.

The same adversity will affect different people in different ways. We have a choice about how we react to events. It is this mental ability to choose which distinguishes people who are more resilient from others who are less.

For example:

Both golf players hit their ball into the trees during a match.

Player 1 responds to the stimulus A with an automatic set of thoughts:

> *"Oh no, not the trees again. I always lose it when the going gets tough, that's just like me. I will probably lose now ..."*

Player 2 responds to exactly the same stimulus with different thoughts:

> *"Oh no, not the trees again! Damn it, but I only just went in, I have to take a penalty here but if I can half this hole I am still in this game. I usually win these close matches ..."*

What do you think the consequences will be?

Another example:

Two women at the theatre hear different things from the same request:

> *"Would anyone mind swapping seats?"*

Woman 1 responds to the stimulus A with an automatic set of thoughts. She has an ingrained belief that everyone is trying to take advantage of her ...

> *"No, that won't be acceptable, I want my seat ..."*

Woman 2 responds to exactly the same stimulus with different thoughts. (She has a strong pattern for wanting to help people ...)

> *"Oh, it doesn't matter – please take my seat."*

Neither knew why the question was being asked.

2.5 **Resilience Inventory**

Try rating yourself on these key factors that resilient people tend to have.

Staying calm under pressure Including expressing emotions in a healthy and constructive way	0 10 ├────┼────┤ **Low** **High**
Controlling your impulses – your ability to delay gratification is a good indication of this	0 10 ├────┼────┤ **Low** **High**
Looking at things optimistically	0 10 ├────┼────┤ **Low** **High**
Accurately identifying the cause of your problems	0 10 ├────┼────┤ **Low** **High**
Empathy with others – how we read people cues to their emotional states	0 10 ├────┼────┤ **Low** **High**
Your faith in your ability to succeed – our sense that we are effective in the world	0 10 ├────┼────┤ **Low** **High**
Taking on challenges and intimacy – reaching out	0 10 ├────┼────┤ **Low** **High**

(Modified from **The Resilience Factor** by Karen Reivich and Andrew Shatte.)

For a more comprehensive assessment and comparison with norms try the free 60 question inventory at www.adaptivlearning.com

So all we need to do is to manage our beliefs and thoughts, which govern how we respond to adversity – sounds easy, doesn't it?

But there is a complicating factor:

- there are certain events that rob us of grace;
- things that push our buttons;
- trigger emotions.

We often do not see reality but react to triggers that release deep emotions form our past. Karen Reivich and Andrew Shatte have some wonderful exercises on detecting **icebergs** and **triggers** in their book, as well as "learning your ABCs and avoiding thinking traps". I recommend that you read their book.

Briefly, an iceberg is something in the present that releases old emotions, so that you react out of all proportion to the event. For example, your spouse might mention something about cleaning your room that triggers an outburst about your own space, that actually links back to how you were treated as a child. You may react over-negatively to people in power in your organisation if you associate their behaviour with people who had power over you in the past, at school say.

Reality

If you are reacting intensely to a situation, it could be a sign that you are being affected by an underlying belief about how the world works and how you need to feel to operate in that world, e.g. "I need to be wary of people taking advantage of me, I need to make sure I get my share."

Can you recognise any of your icebergs?

Self-awareness of icebergs and internal triggers to our emotions is an important development of emotional regulation and empathy. The more you can calm your own voices, the better you can empathise and really hear what the client is saying.

By asking open questions that challenge the client to think below the surface structure of their language, you can release underlying meanings even from very matter of fact answers, for example:

"How are your team doing?"

"So, they are not very effective at the moment. What do you see happening?"

"What does 'behind target' mean?"

"Which aspects of the job are they most behind with?"

etc.

This moving from surface structure of language and beliefs explains why clients can find the process very challenging and very valuable. Remember the ESRC research that found that the most important feature clients cited was a "partnership style" marked by a willingness to challenge the client along with openness and integrity.

Another way to build your self-awareness is to become conscious of your common thinking traps.

2.6 **Thinking traps**

Aaron Beck, a cognitive therapist, suggested 7 thinking traps that make people susceptible to depression. (It is a thinking trap when there is little evidence to support the conclusion.)

Jumping to conclusions   "We need to do this." (Solutioneering)

Tunnel vision   your mind automatically taking short cuts; and not seeing the bigger picture

Magnifying and minimising glass half empty/glass half full

Personalising   attribute problems to one's own doing

Externalising   "No-one can sell in this market."

Over-generalising   "That bad shot means I will never be able to do it."

Mind reading   believing that we know what those around us are thinking, and acting accordingly

An effective consultant needs a level of self-awareness to be successful in the role. This includes recognising your own personality preferences via tools like Myers Briggs and how you react to pressure. The more self-aware you are, the more you will be able to engage with your client; flex your style to build rapport; see the reality behind problems; and help your client face up to that reality as a trusted partner.

How to build your resilience

How you react to an event (Adversity) will depend on your self-awareness and how the event triggers your in-built triggers, beliefs and icebergs, leading you to adopt possible thinking traps.

One of the first things you can do is to identify your ABCs or what pushes your buttons.

List common events that stimulate a reaction in you, for example:

- unfair performance rating in appraisal
- clients turning up late to meetings

Adversity	Belief	Consequences

Now, on the same grid, add the common beliefs and thoughts that are triggered within you, for example:

Adversity	Belief
e.g. unfair performance rating in appraisal	I never get my fair rating
Clients turning up late to meetings	They do not respect me

And then add the usual emotional and behavioural consequences, for example:

Adversity	Belief	Consequences
Unfair performance rating in appraisal	I never get my fair rating	Anger, I tend to go quiet and passive, sullen, meeting does not go well, resentment. I do not hear the feedback which might help me.
Clients turning up late to meetings	They do not respect me	I rush to the task-part of the meeting and miss out on relationship building and feel resentful

Can you recognise what thinking traps you are falling into?

Jumping to conclusions (solutioneering)

Tunnel vision your mind automatically taking short cuts and not seeing the bigger picture

Magnifying and minimising glass half empty/glass half full

Personalising attribute problems to one's own doing

Externalising   "No one can sell in this market."

Over-generalising   "That bad shot means I will never be able to do it."

Mind reading   believing that we know what those around us are thinking, and acting accordingly

e.g. average performance rating in appraisal	I never get my fair rating	Anger, I tend to go quiet and passive, sullen, meeting does not go well, resentment	**Personalising** **Over-generalising**
Clients turning up late to meetings	They do not respect me	I rush to the task-part of the meeting and miss out on relationship building, feel resentful	**Jumping to conclusions** **Personalising** **Mind reading** There might be a genuine reason for lateness

2.7 **Hints on how to avoid thinking traps**

Jumping to conclusions

You get a message that the client wants to talk to you. You might jump to conclusions, e.g. "Oh no, what has gone wrong now? I wonder if the training was delivered on time? Is she angry about xxx?" How do you respond more resiliently?

- **Gather more data**: Spend a few minutes checking on recent deliverables to the client – is anything due? What has happened recently?
- **Talk to yourself**: "At the moment I have no evidence that this message is about anything wrong."

If you assume that something is wrong, you won't really listen in an open-minded way when you talk to the client. But by countering your thinking trap you will be better able to be in control, ask an open question and listen carefully to what the real issue is. You will also be in a calmer state, ready to tackle any issues that come up.

Tunnel vision

e.g. "Oh no, this presentation is going badly, everyone is fidgeting!"

You are focusing on only the negative information in the room, and screening out other contradictory information to your beliefs. (There may be another reason for the fidgeting.) How do you respond more resiliently?

- **Gather more data**: What has happened recently? What is the temperature?
- **Talk to yourself**: "At the moment I have no evidence that this message is about anything wrong with my presentation. What am I missing?"

Magnifying and minimising

This is about being over-positive or negative given the same information. How do you respond more resiliently?

- **Gather more data**: "What are the facts?"
- **Talk to yourself**: "I may be over/under playing this?"

Personalising

This is about attributing problems to one's own doing, e.g. "That was a poor golf shot, I am useless", whereas your playing colleague just notices that it was a difficult downhill lie. How do you respond more resiliently?

- **Gather more data**: "Why do you think I did that?"
- **Talk to yourself**: "I am playing okay, I just didn't account for the downhill lie."

Externalising

This is the opposite of personalising, e.g. "The wind blew it out!" Seen as an ABC, the externalisers avoid immediate sadness and protect their self-image but instead may find themselves prone to anger. How do you respond more resiliently?

- **Gather more data**: "How strong is this wind? Could it have blown it out?"
- **Talk to yourself**: "Why am I getting angry – the wind is the same for everyone, I will just have to adapt."

Over-generalising

You may think "I am a bad consultant" when the facts might say otherwise. How do you respond more resiliently?

- **Gather more data**: "I will ask my clients what they value from me."
- **Talk to yourself**: "I am over-generalising from one impression."

Mind reading

You may think "He never arrives on time, he doesn't respect me" when perhaps he is always late for other peoples meetings too. Gain further information before jumping into your trap. How do you respond more resiliently?

- **Gather more data**: "I will ask colleagues if he is always late for them, and ask the client why he is late."
- **Talk to yourself**: "I do not know why he is late."

General principles for how to respond more resiliently
- Pause;
- Hold back from jumping into your trap;
- Search for data;
- Break the situation into A.B.C;
- Ask yourself: "What is real?"

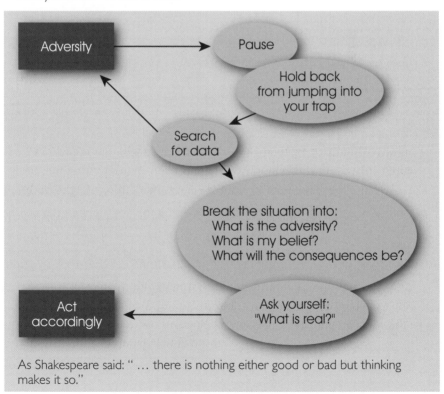

As Shakespeare said: " ... there is nothing either good or bad but thinking makes it so."

2.8 **An example of the need for resilience when working as an internal consultant.**

I thought you might find it helpful to read some reflections from a real consulting intervention. At the least, it might help you to see that consulting is not a game of perfect. In reality, you will come up against obstacles and self-doubt, which you will need to continuously self-manage.

The unfairness of it all and the need to be resilient

At the moment I am working as an internal consultant on a large internal project for a multinational company. The Training Director has asked for me to join the change team in order to complete a performance analysis and specify any learning solutions needed.

One month into the project I have **not** been able to:

- Meet the client;
- Run any of the planned analysis workshops;
- Gain useful access to the target group.

Despite these setbacks, and although I have been keeping the client informed of the delays, I have heard through one of the project managers that the client had been asking when I would be delivering the e-learning.

My feelings are:

- Frustration that I have not been able to build any relationship with the client;
- Annoyance that she was expecting e-learning solutions when I can see no need for any;
- Anger that she seemed to think that I could magically invent solutions without any access to the target groups!
- Inadequacy that I cannot manage their expectations better.

My thoughts are:

- They do not respect me;
- They are expecting magic.

This brought back memories of inadequacy and failure at school.

My self-talk goes something like this:
- "I have been successful in the past."
- "Why are they behaving like this?"
- "What are the facts?"
- "I am probably imagining lots of terrible things that are not true."

So what are the facts?
- Client fails to respond to emails about the original contract;
- I find out that she has been dragged into another business-critical project, which has taken priority over this one;
- She eventually apologises that she has been a bottleneck; explains that she is too busy; and delegates the project to a junior project manager.

The clients seemed quite happy, mainly because they had avoided any investigation of the real problems, yet they were also pressurising me for my solutions. They were avoiding the problem, but treating me as an expert and wanting an instant solution. I can feel all these projected assumptions. When I try to get more information about the performance gap, I am referred to other documents; or they suggest that I should know the information already and I am wasting their valuable time. They pick me up on spelling mistakes and incorrect acronyms. No one wants to re-examine the problem.

My internal dialogue (ABCs) to this "adversity" goes something like this:
- I cannot spell;
- I am not good at detail;
- Can I really add any value here?
- They are frustrated with me because I keep hassling them;
- They will throw me off the project;
- They are probably talking behind my back about how incompetent I am.

So I have to talk to myself:

- Is there any evidence for the above?
- What are the facts?
- I have been successful before.
- It is not me but them.
- They are defensive and do not want to look at the problem.
- What can I do to manage the relationship and build rapport?

Today I am feeling a little better. I have found out that the client is actually a contractor like myself, and none of the project team knows much about the real performers or the performance gap. They feel defensive and committed to tight delivery deadlines.

I have asked the assistant to set up a face-to-face meeting with the client. I am going to find out about her needs and build rapport with her before I do any more analysis. I will also contact the Training Director and keep him informed about the delays to the project so that I am not exposed to criticism.

I know that I have been successful on similar projects in the past. It is not me.

Now that I have access to the client, I need to listen to her and trust my skills to build rapport and help her with the project problems.

I have also found out from other people that she is very systematic and logical, so I will flex my behaviour accordingly …

I must go back and build rapport and gain trust before moving on to the task part of the project.

I hope this gives you a glimpse of what may be going on under the surface of the calm, collected consultant.

Working with people is complex. As an internal consultant you do not have the luxury of being able to blame others and resort to defence mechanisms. You have to tackle the problem, which also includes your own reactions to adversity. When you can do this you can help others to perform and become a respected business partner.

44

Summary

- To be a successful business partner, you need a number of attributes.
- We all differ in our ability to deal with setbacks.
- Building competence is the key to developing psychological resilience.
- We are not in control of events:
  - **We will experience** Adversity (**A**)
  - But we can influence our beliefs (**B**)
    - Which governs the consequences (**C**) and the behavioural and emotional results
- Certain events trigger deep emotions in us (icebergs) and we may react inappropriately (thinking traps).
- Being aware of your A, B, C's, triggers, icebergs and thinking traps can help you become more resilient.

3

The performance consulting process

Contents

Note:

If you have already read "Improving Employee Performance" you might want to skip quickly through this part.

3.1 **Introducing the process**

The Chief Executive explained a problem to her two best business partners:

"Our middle managers are not creative enough. Can you do something to help them?"

Business partner one commissioned an expert on creativity to run a creativity workshop at enormous cost. Six months later the Chief Executive challenged the business partner:

"Our sales are still down compared with the competition. The press say our products are stale and haven't changed for years! What good did that training do?"

In contrast, **business partner two** asked some questions:

Business partner two: "What would it look like if the managers were more creative?"

Chief Executive: "Our product range would be fresher for a start."

Business partner two: "How would you measure this?"

Chief Executive: "Our competitors have 40% of their range as new products for this season. Our figure is 15%."

Business partner two: "What would be the effect if we do nothing?"

Chief Executive: "Our sales figures will continue to fall, these consultants are under threat and so is my job!"

Business partner two explains his successful solutions:

"Well, I didn't accept that the problem was the creativity of our managers. Instead I got them together and presented the problem. They were amazed that there was a difference in their product refresh rate compared with their competitors. They thought the Chief Executive wanted to see continuity and had often given the subtle message that she did not want too much change."

"I facilitated a session where they came with their own action plan. The Chief Executive had been solutioneering, all she had done was give us her version of the solution."

Business partner two solved the problem rather than implementing an instant solution. The only way to guarantee success is to understand the causes of the performance problem and implement integrated solutions.

3.2 **The 7-step process**

There are several problem-solving processes. I have distilled these into a simple 7-step process:

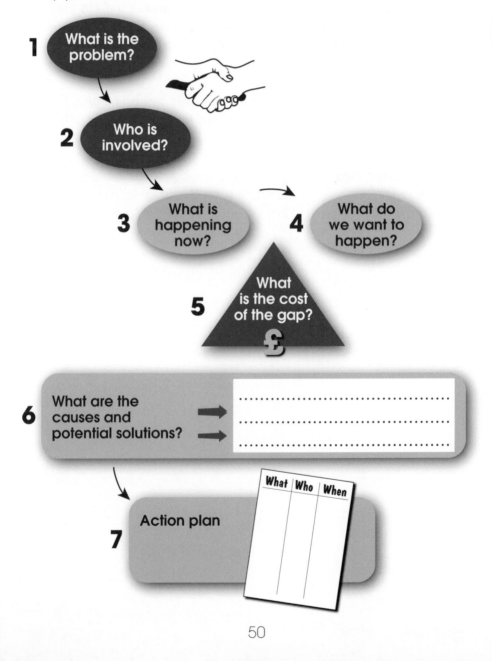

3.3 **A simple example**

You can use the 7-step process to solve any performance problem. Let's start with an apparently simple personal problem.

How to improve Mike's fitness

Mike is one of your friends who wants to improve his fitness. Business partner one would probably just say: 'Join a gym, Mike!' Business partner two, on the other hand, would take some time to ask a few questions, get to the bottom of the problem and produce real solutions that are more likely to work.

Mike describes the problem to be solved as "How to get that run in every day?" Using the 7-step process, the first thing to do is to find out **who is involved**.

Mike identifies five key people:

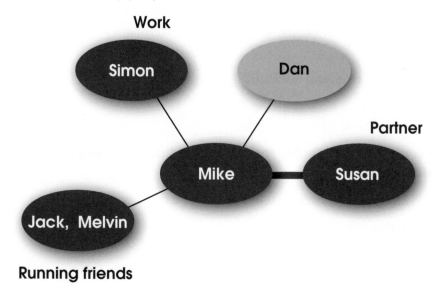

Secondly, business partner two will **have a conversation** with Mike, which goes something like this:

So, Mike, what is happening now?

- "I haven't got time to go running – work and studying get greater priority."
- "I run when I am at home, but it is only once a week and I don't find that acceptable."

What do you want to be able to do?

- "I would like to do a run every day!"

How big would you say the gap is between what you would like to do and what is actually happening now?

- "I feel very frustrated."
- "I miss out on having a healthy body and a healthy mind."
- "Running would help me to focus on my studying."

Is the cost of this gap serious?

- "Yes, I want to do something about it!"

Let's see if we can identify the causes for this gap and some possible solutions.

We will ask questions around whether Mike has the:

Knowledge
Skill
Motivation
Environment

needed to close the gap.

Knowledge

- Do you lack some knowledge?

Skill

- Do you lack some skill?
- Were you once able to do it?
- Have you got the capability to learn how to do this?

Motivation

- Do you get feedback on your performance?
- If you do it right, do other people suffer in any way, e.g. time spent running means you do not see Susan?
- Are you being rewarded for low performance?
- Do you lack the self-esteem to solve this?

Environment

- Is there anything wrong with your environment, methods and equipment?
- Is Susan helping?
- Are there any other obstacles?

In Mike's case the questions went like this:

Do you know about running?
Yes, I think so.

Have you got the skills to do it?
Yes.

Can we make the performance easier in any way?
I could aim for 3 times per week instead of every day.

Can you use a checklist?
Yes, I will mark mornings on the calendar when I can run and when I do run.

Did you once run every day?
Yes, I used to run with Jack and Melvin but I could try to find people who want to run at lunchtime at work.

If you do more running do you suffer in any way?
No, if I run I feel better able to handle the work and my course. Every day takes a lot of time though. I will reward myself for achieving my running targets.

If you do not go for a run do you benefit in any way?
Yes, if I do not go for a run I can have dinner with Susan. I will ask Susan if she would mind eating dinner later.

Does it really matter to you?
Yes, it does. I will find a club and run with colleagues.

Do you fear failure?
I will be realistic and do what I can.

Is there anything wrong with your environment, methods and equipment?
Yes, I need some new shoes.

Will Susan playing her part help you to perform?
I will ask Susan to support me and promise a meal out when I reach my study and running targets.

Are there any other obstacles stopping you?
There are no showers at work – I will see if we can arrange something.

So what are you going to do then, Mike? Write down your ideas in this action plan.

What	Who	When
The new shoes will have to wait until pay day	Me	Next month
I will talk to Susan tonight and set up the calendar	Susan and me	Tonight
I will find out about joining a club with some colleagues from work	See Jim	This lunchtime
I will run before I start studying	Me	Tonight

What happened when we analysed Mike's problem?

1. We looked at **who was involved**.
2. We looked at **what is happening now**.
3. We looked at **what he wants to happen**.
4. We checked that the **gap was worth doing something about**:
    – Is the cost of this gap serious?
    – "Yes, I want to do something about it."

5. We investigated the **possible reasons** why Mike is finding it hard to get that run in every day:
    – **K**nowledge, **S**kills, **M**otivation and **E**nvironment.

6. These questions raised several **possible solutions**.
7. We selected the immediate ones in an **action plan**.

This is the 7-step process in action.

Lessons from the running example

Are you surprised about what is involved in really understanding how to improve Mike's fitness? By working through his performance gap and all the causes we came up with a range of solutions. If you put them all together in an action plan with dates on it, Mike might actually start running again.

Many of the factors were motivational and environmental – but they were mixed up. I hope you can see the need for a systematic approach to analysing what is going on.

Lessons:

- Problems never involve only one person: they always involve the interaction of people within a system.
- Solutions to performance problems are often not radical. Your client may just need time to think it through logically.
- Solutions often involve groups of actions rather than one big, magic solution.
- The assumed problem is often not the real problem at all.
- Facing up to your problems is the first step in solving them.

What lessons did you learn from the example? Ready to try it yourself? To get started, use the checklist on the next few pages.

Think of a problem that you have right now

This is an opportunity to get some immediate value from the process. Choose a relatively simple personal issue, such as "How do I..."

- keep fit?
- make more time for my family?
- get the builders to finish the extension?
- cope with my in-laws this weekend?

3.4 **The 7-step checklist**

Step 1 – What is the problem?

- What is the problem as the client sees it?
- How long have they got for this meeting?
- What are they expecting to get out of this meeting?

Step 2 – Who is involved?

- Draw a diagram of all the people involved in the problem.
- Put the key people in the centre.
- Make links between the key people.
- Label what is happening between them.

Step 3 – What is happening now?

How is the system performing? Try to get facts, figures, anything measurable.

[ ]

What are the key people doing now?

[ ]

What is the client doing now?

[ ]

Step 4 – What do we want to happen?

Visualise how you would like things to be. How is the system performing?

[ ]

What are the key people doing?

[ ]

What effect does this have on the client?

[ ]

Step 5 – What is the cost of the gap?

What would happen if you did nothing? Calculate the cost.

[ ]

Is it worth doing something about?

Ideas generator

Step 6 – What are the causes and potential solutions?

Try to generate as many solutions as possible. Suspend judgement as to their feasibility, and write them all down.

What do the key players lack?

Knowledge or skill	Idea
Do they lack some knowledge?	Give them the knowledge (just tell them)?
Do they lack some knowledge and skill?	Make the performance easier in some way by: • Simplifying the tasks? • Splitting the job? • Designing checklists? • Clarifying performance standards?
Were they once able to do it?	Try practice, better information and feedback.
Have they got the capability to learn how to do this?	Consider training them and providing learning materials.
If they haven't got the capability…	Can we transfer them to a job that they can do or terminate their employment?

Motivation

Do they get feedback on performance?	Provide clear goals and regular feedback on positive as well as negative performance.
If they do it right, do they suffer in any way, e.g. by being given more work?	Reduce the punishment for high performance. Introduce rewards and incentives.
Are they being rewarded for low performance?	Stop the rewards.
Do people lack self-esteem?	Help them visualise success, set positive goals. Catch people doing things right, build on success.

Environment

Is there anything wrong with their environment, methods, equipment?	Improve.
Are the managers helping?	Improve management.
Any other obstacles?	Try to remove them.

Possible solutions: list them here

Look at your list of possible solutions.

Cross out those:

- that are just not feasible;
- whose cost would be greater than the benefit.

Highlight those:

- that can be easily implemented;
- that will give the best results for minimum effort.

Step 7 – Action plan

Now decide on the immediate actions to do first.

What?	Who?	When?

Set a date to evaluate whether the performance gap has closed.

$$\_\_/\_\_/\_\_$$

Summary

The 7-step process allows you to move from an "order taker" role to "joint problem solving".

In order to do this you need to ask the client some questions about the original performance problem.

The 7 steps are:

1. What is the problem
2. Who is involved
3. What is happening now
4. What do we want to happen
5. What is he cost of the gap
6. What are the causes and potential solutions
7. Action plan

Even a simple example like improving Mike's fitness involves:

- Several people;
- Analysis of the performance gap;
- Several solutions.

Solutions to performance problems are often not radical. Your client may just need time to think it through logically.

Often the assumed problem is not the real problem at all.

Facing up to your problems is the first step to solving them.

Now let's look at the steps in more detail.

Thinking of the 7-step process in a new way

In the previous chapter we looked at the process as 7 steps. To understand the process as a whole, it helps if we split it into 3 phases:

A. BUILDING TRUST AND RAPPORT
B. FACING UP TO THE PROBLEM
C. BUILDING POWERFUL SOLUTIONS

In each phase you will interact differently with your client:

- At the start of the meeting it is about **BUILDING TRUST AND RAPPORT** and your behaviour is non-threatening and open.
- In the middle phase of the process we need to be much more challenging because we are **FACING UP TO THE PROBLEM**.
- Finally the mood changes again in **BUILDING POWERFUL SOLUTIONS** and moving into action.

These overlay the 7-steps (see next page).

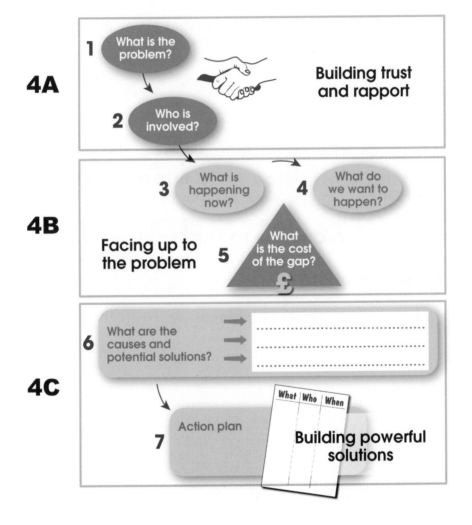

64

Building trust and rapport

Contents

4A Building trust and rapport

At the start of the meeting your client will have an idea of their problem and probably solutions in their head. They want to know that you will listen to their ideas and that they can trust you to help them. **Your behaviour needs to be non-threatening and open**.

You will be:

- listening to the client;
- mapping out the system that performs;
- drawing a rich picture of the problem;
- helping the client understand their own situation;
- showing that you understand it;
- moving to joint problem-solving (sitting side-by-side);
- keeping the problem fluid;
- dealing with emotions before you get down to the task.

On the introductory skills workshop we tend to suggest that everything happens in the meeting with the client. In reality, you can, and should, do as much work beforehand as possible. Let's assume that this is a first meeting with a new client.

A1 **Before you meet the client**

You need to think about:
- building your credibility;
- finding out about them as a person;
- doing some research into their situation.

Building your credibility

One of the first things you will have to do is to convince the client that you are worth speaking to: Who are you? What experience do you have? Why am I talking to you?

So have your credentials ready:
- Qualifications
- Experience
- Common ground with the client

Ask your boss to sell you in before the meeting and to explain your credentials.

Find out as much about the client as possible:
- what do they think of your department?
- have they had good service in the past?
- how does this client behave?

Be aware of yourself

The first step towards building rapport with others is to be self-aware. What sort of person are you?
- Are you energised by external or internal factors?
- Do you pay attention to information step-by-step, or can you see the big picture and make intuitive leaps?
- Do you make decisions based on your feeling or thoughts?
- Do you plan things or wing it?

This is my short hand version of the Myers Briggs personality types.

Extraversion/**I**ntroversion

(Drawing energy from the external or internal world)

Sensing/**IN**tuition

(Taking information through facts and detail or intuitive leaps and the big picture)

Thinking/**F**eeling

(Decisions based on logic or values)

Judging/**P**erceiving

(Planned and organised or spontaneous and flexible)

If you have not already done this, I recommend some self-analysis (see the bibliography for references). The principle is that if you are more aware of your preferences you are more likely to be sensitive to the preferences of others. With skill, you can still be yourself but flex your style to work more effectively with others.

Find out about them as a person

We all have our own system for "reading" or categorising the people that we meet.

How self-aware are you? What system do you use to categorise people? Again, I tend to use a simplified version of Myers Briggs:

What sort of preferences do they have?

- Are they energised by external or internal factors?
- Do they pay attention to information step-by-step or see the big picture and make intuitive leaps?
- Do they make decisions based on feeling or thoughts?
- Do they plan things or wing it?

Or (an even simpler categorisation) are they:

- Head or heart?
- Detail or big picture?
- Intuitive or logical?

Or, in a simple Neuro-Linguistic Programming (NLP) classification:

- Reactive – pro-active;
- Away from motivation – towards motivation;
- Internal focus – external focus;
- Procedural – options.

I hope you can see some common themes in these classifications.

We are not trying to complete a personality profile of your client – it is enough just to start thinking about their preferences. This will make you more sensitive to their preferred way of working and can, for example, help you to work more effectively together.

For example:

Martin works for an advertising agency – he will always arrive late for the meeting, ignore the agenda, want to catch up with the gossip, and then move quickly on to exciting ideas to solve the problem.

How do you work with him?

Probably you will have to drive the agenda and keep him on track.

Whereas:

Carol is a senior scientist for a drug company – she arrives on time, likes an agenda and does not want any chitchat. She just wants to know the background before she moves through the task in a sequential fashion.

How do you behave with her?

I would say what you want to before she moves you on to the next task!

To work better with any type of person we need to establish rapport and trust. A quick way to start is to establish any common ground.

What you wear is important

Try to dress similarly to your client, or be aware of the statement that you are making by your dress, for example:

In Martin's advertising agency the unofficial dress code seems to be designer jeans, very expensive shirts with cuff links and designer shoes. *As an internal consultant* you may choose more formal trousers, but perhaps wear similar shirts with cuff links?

In Carol's drug company she wears predominantly black and the men wear suites and ties. *As a consultant* you may choose to wear a suit with a tie?

The principle is the same – be yourself but flex your behaviour slightly to help the client feel comfortable with you and build rapport. Being aware of your dress and the impression you make is all part of your self-awareness, which will give you options in your consulting. The more aware you are of subtle non-verbal messages, the more successful you will be in building rapport, and the more sensitive and successful you will be with the client.

For example, one of my clients is very annoyed by people who do not use proper pens, have scruffy briefcases and even wear shoes without leather soles. I do not change my shoes but I am careful to be smart and use a proper pen when we are working together.

Homework

Finally, before you meet the client, do your homework – do you have any common ground?

- People you know?
- Previous employers?
- Sporting interests?
- Family?

How to confront "ghosts"

Before you start a meeting you may be able to anticipate the client's reactions to you from previous experience of your department, predecessor or colleagues. They may have been disappointed in the service from your organisation before or have heard unrealistic expectations of your ability to deliver.

How do you handle these?

You need to tackle these concerns before you move on to the task. So confront them upfront:

"I have been here x months. I have heard that we failed to meet your expectations on the last project we delivered for you, can you tell me about that?"

"What was it about our delivery that caused you the most problems?"

"What do you need us to do to make sure this does not happen again?"

Do your homework before you meet the client …

A2 **When you meet the client**

The first two minutes of any meeting are very important. The client will be "reading" you.

- Believe that you deserve to be there;
- *Arrive* in the room – stand and absorb the atmosphere before you start.
- Keep eye contact with the client;
- Match what they do with their body language;
- Match what they do with their voice.

A typical rapport building session

Keith the CEO of Toni Music meets John the new business partner for the first time:

K: "Good to meet you, John. Angela tells me good things about you – how long have you been with Toni Music?"

J: "I have been here six months and before that I was senior business partner for Roxy Music. I think you know Ted Hughes, one of my clients who I did some successful projects for?"

(As Keith has stood up to meet John he matches his body posture, firm handshake and eye contact. As an experienced operator Keith will be trying to "read" John. It is up to you to manage the impression you give as someone who has credibility and can add value to your client and also as someone who will be helpful and emotionally comfortable to be with.)

I know it sounds corny but you have to do it!

- Find common ground;
- State your credentials;
- Show your connections with powerful people they respect.

But be genuine – there is no point in feigning an interest in golf if you have never played!

73

A3 What happens when you do not trust your client?

The majority of your performance consulting meetings will be successful if you use a rational joint problem solving approach and even powerful, manipulative people will change their behaviour if you are open and honest. If you are in a supportive meeting these people are usually carried along with the group ethos and will not expose themselves. However there will be times when people are playing games.

You might notice this from your feelings at the time:

- Things don't feel quite right;
- You don't really trust what someone is saying;
- One person is speaking too much and with too much intensity.

Trust your feelings – you are probably right, there may well be something going on below the apparent interactions. The secret is to be sensitive and trust your feelings, and then use this awareness to choose how to react in a flexible way.

If things don't feel right you may be in a negotiation rather than a straightforward meeting. Fundamentally, there are two sorts of negotiation:

1. Rational joint problem-solving;
2. Bargaining.

Rational joint problem-solving

There is no problem here because the 7-step process is a rational joint problem-solving process which will help you to resolve any problem. The important thing to emphasise in joint problem-solving is your joint goal, and then agree to use a rational process to move towards it.

How do I get "buy in" to working in joint problem-solving?

Keeping in mind the idea that people in key roles need to feel that they made the decision, one good way to win over stakeholders is to invite them to a problem analysis session, where you take the stakeholders through the process to analyse the problem from their perspective and agree action.

This works very well if you can get all the stakeholders in a room together. The practical things to remember are:

- Allow enough space – book a big room with a blank wall;
- Allow plenty of time, 2 to 3 hours for 3 to 4 people;
- Remove the tables and place the chairs in a semi-circle facing the blank wall;
- Stick flip charts on the wall showing the 7-step process headings;
- At the start make sure you encourage rapport between people with an introductions exercise;
- You may fill in some of the flip charts with your current thinking but leave the solutions and action plan blank so that the team can make their own decisions.

By the end of the session all the stakeholders should buy in to the agreed action plan.

What is game playing?

At this early stage of the relationship the client may try to play games with you. They may use a powerful position to get you to promise more than you ought to.

> *"I am sure that we will have no problems now that you are our business partner, Dean."*

> *"I just need you to commit to all the sales force being trained by April."*

> *"Training is the number one priority in our business plan this year."*

Watch out for praise and sweeping solutions that **you** have to deliver! They may be setting you up in a game called NIGYSOB ("Now I have Got You, You Son Of a Bitch"). Eric Berne describes this in **Games People Play**, a very accessible book describing Freudian theory about our personality and ego states in terms of:

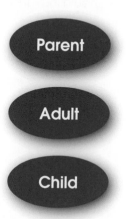

Berne called his theory Transactional Analysis, partly because he saw effective communication between people as straightforward transactions. For example, when you are in a child state (having fun) and relate to others in a child state, this is an appropriate transaction.

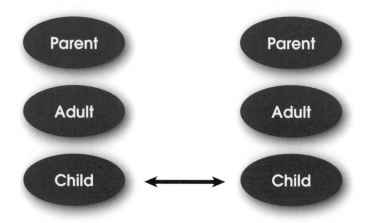

However, Berne saw that interactions could also be crossed, e.g. a "parent" message from someone:

"Keep you shoes shiny, young man"

could **hook** a "child" reaction of:

"Push off Granddad!"

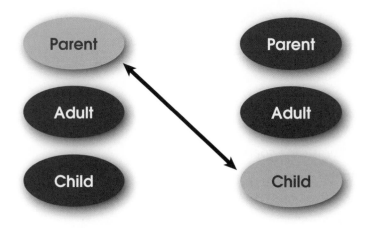

The "ideal" state for effective communication at work is Adult – Adult.

Berne also explains how many transactions are deliberately crossed and manipulative. He calls these psychological games.

NIGYSOB – Now I have Got You, You Son Of a Bitch

This is when someone praises you and sets you up to take full responsibility for a task:

"Yes Chris, we selected you for this important project because you are excellent at handling these special difficulties."

NIGYSOB is often associated with expecting you to be a "pair of hands" consultant or order taker:

"We need the solution ready by April for the launch of the new product. Your predecessor could not have met such tight deadlines but we are sure that, with your ability, you can manage it."

Can you think of any times when you have been set up in this way? Game playing is deliberate manipulation. Do you recognise any of these "games"?

"Poor Me" (I will never be able to do it)

"Ain't It Awful" (We will never be able to do it because verything is awful)

"Why Don't You – Yes But" (Yes but..)

"See What You Made Me Do" (It's your fault)

"Let's You and Him Fight" (Keep me out of it).

Or ...

"I've got no time."

"The systems can't cope."

"No money."

"We would have to change too much."

"It is unrealistic."

"We have tried that and it did not work."

"Senior managers will not buy into it."

"It might work there but our culture is different."

Some of the consultants that I train complain about feeling "steamrollered". Their clients often refer to a person with power as "X says", giving the impression that the solution has already been decided and cannot be questioned. They are passing you a non-negotiable order, e.g. "X (our common boss) says we need this, when can you deliver?" or "The board wants to see this by April, I am sure that you can deliver". Both of these are examples of referring to power and treating you as an order taker.

A5   Coping with games playing and manipulation

Now isn't it a bit paranoid to be talking in this way? Surely organisations are rational/adult places and this sort of thing does not happen?

Even though all organisations have an adult, rational, purposeful surface, as a consultant it is important to recognise the hidden organisation. All organisations are emotional, irrational, power-ridden places.

Power has been called the last dirty secret of the organisation.

Luckily the best way to deal with the games playing and manipulation is to:

1. Recognise when it is happening;

2. React in a rational/adult way;

3. Try to bring the interaction back to adult – adult by your behaviour.

Before we can move on to joint collaboration, we need to have built up a level of rapport and trust in our relationship. This means that you also need to trust your client.

It is at the very start of the meeting that you need to look out for psychological games and set-ups.

These set-ups can be innocent: the client may just have been brought up in the organisational culture that expects your department to be subservient deliverers of instant solutions with no questions asked!

The client may think that a business partner is just another supplier, and that when she asks for a "Customer Relationship Management (CRM) package", without any reference to the underlying problems, she just needs you to help her clarify her own requirements. Most people are in this category and by altering your behaviour to challenge and define the performance problem, you build respect and power as a valued partner.

BUT

Some managers are so attached to their powerful positions that they find it very difficult to accept any challenge from you, a lower status supplier, and they react in a parental way, preventing you from understanding the real performance problem.

The may have their own reasons for wanting a quick fix, and will move the spotlight from them to you, wanting to avoid any exposure of the current performance gap with their team!

My advice is that it is hard to change another person's behaviour but you can change your own.

Start all new relationships on a rational, authentic basis and the client will usually react in a similar way, for example:

Clarify your role

"My role is to work with you to make sure we can deliver solutions that meet your requirements."

Explain the process you will use

"In order to make sure that we meet your requirement, we have a process to make sure that we are crystal clear about it before we commission any solutions."

"My job is to work with you to check your requirements. I will bring in other specialists as necessary."

Finally move to physical rapport by asking:

"Can we start to map out who will use this CRM package?"

At the same time, produce a blank sheet of paper and intimate that this is where you want to record the information.

81

Push it across the desk or ask:

"Can we sit here so we can draw it together?"

Be authentic; explain why you are doing this:

"So that I have a good idea of who needs this solution."

These stages can be used to move someone away from "solutioneering" – you can move to sitting side-by-side which encourages joint problem-solving.

In most cases the client will be happy to investigate the problem and work rationally.

If the client responds negatively, you now have a different interaction to manage and you will have to alter your behaviour to be more defensive:

- If they are playing games you need to try to get them back to adult – adult.
- If they are playing power, you may have to retort with power and treat the meeting as a bargaining negotiation (although you need to be ready to quit the meeting).
- Sometimes you might agree to give the client what they want (if it does not cost too much and will not do harm).
- Sometimes you will just have to accept that the client is not ready for a joint problem-solving relationship.

In all cases you need to handle the emotional relationship before moving on to the task.

There is no magic answer for how to deal with game playing; the use and abuse of power; and manipulation.

Some tips:

- Read up about games so that you can spot them;
- Trust your feelings – if something feels "a bit off", it probably is;
- Don't react emotionally;

- Stop the conversation if you recognise that you are getting angry or disturbed and cannot work out why;
- Listen to your thoughts – "This sounds too good to be true";
- React in an adult way;
- Ask questions;
- Keep things rational – stick to facts;
- If you are in a game – do something different;
- Get out of the interaction – make some excuse and give yourself time to reflect on what has been going on. Discuss it with a friend;
- Read Chapter 2 on building resilience.

I think you will recognise that there is a whole world of study here. Luckily, in business we are usually dealing with rational, explicit relationships. Just keep your eyes and feelings open to when things are not going as you would expect. Trust your feelings: watch out for games and misuse of power but stay true to your values and normal consulting behaviours. If things are still not working then bale out, win some time to discuss the relationship with a colleague that you trust. Get a second opinion and re-plan your interventions with this particular client.

In general, anything you can do to build your self-awareness, to understand your patterns and triggers, will help you to be more aware of other people's behaviour and motivations. (See Chapter 5.) The more aware you are of what is really happening in meetings (behind the words), the more power you will have to flex your behaviour and achieve successful results.

How to stay in an "Adult" frame of mind

Eric Berne's theory can explain the inner dialogue that we sometimes have in our heads:

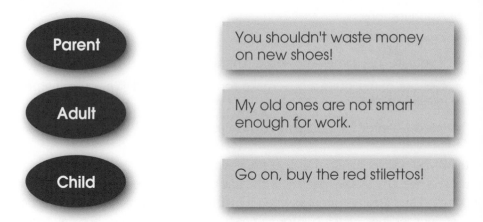

Our voices, or ego-states, run a constant bargaining between our different selves to keep ourselves sane. Eric Berne suggested that we engage others by transactions with their ego states. This is fine when they are complimentary:

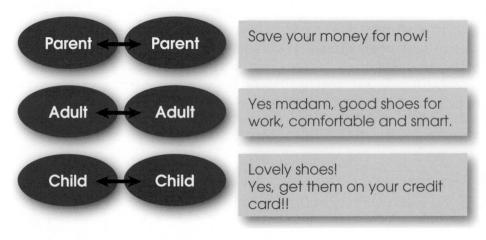

Eric Berne suggests problems occur when we get crossed transactions:

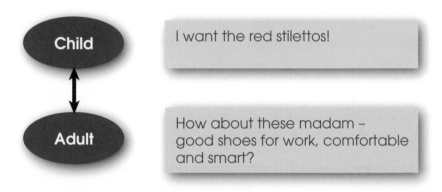

This can happen in organisations – this sort of "Parental" order can hook your "Parent" or "Child".

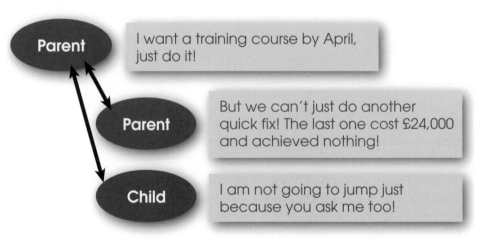

If you find that you are reacting as either angry child or angry parent, then you are giving away much of your power in the relationship and you are being manipulated by the other person.

A7 Power play – negotiation

The other main form of meeting is when your client is using power and a bargaining stance. They want to get as much from you as possible whilst giving the least away.

The simplest use of power is the power to say "Just do what I say!" This can be a very straightforward "Just do it!", or it can be after a period of pretend listening, after which they state their previous ideas again.

Client	Your response
"Just do it!"	"It may not be the best solution."
I want to create the appearance of action – "Just do it!"	This quick fix will not work – "What is the problem we are trying to solve?"
It is not an important project for me, it does not warrant my attention – "Just do it!"	"?!"

The key thing in situations like this is to recognise that **you are not in joint problem-solving so rational argument will not work**!

The only things that work with a power player are opposing power or compliance. You are in a **bargaining** meeting, where the decision over action will depend on who has the most power, **not** on what is the best thing to do.

In this case you need to calculate your power versus the client.

Client	Your internal dialogue
"Just do it!"	• It may not be the best solution. • My boss will never support me. • I have no evidence that this quick fix has not worked elsewhere . • I need this job. • He plays golf with the Chairman. • I will look as if I am slowing things down. • He has more power than me. • This quick fix will only cost £2,000. • I will go along with it and use it as an opportunity to find out about the real performance gap.
	"Okay."

Or

Client	Your internal dialogue
"Just do it!"	• It may not be the best solution. • I could escalate this to my boss? • I have evidence that this quick fix has not worked in other instances. • I play golf with the Chairman. • He is on dodgy ground. • This quick fix will cost £100k.
	"I will challenge him."

How much power do you have?

Try drawing a map of the key people in your world. You may think it is just you and the client, but what about your supporters and theirs?

Everyone works within a system. Who are your supporters? Where are your alliances? Where are theirs and how strong are they? Use larger objects to denote more power and put people in relation to each other, for example:

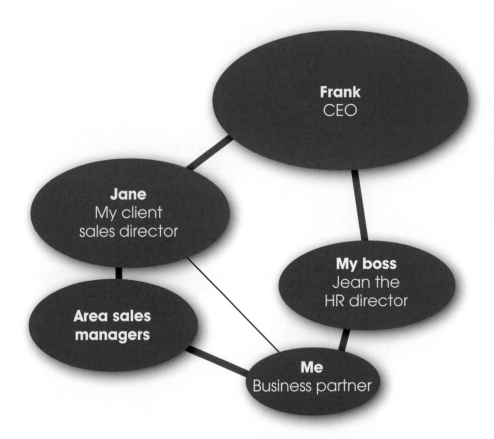

In this case, the business partner has very little power, but Frank might be the most useful ally, especially because of his strong links with Jean.

If you decide to use your power, then you could be into a bargaining negotiation, where the first person makes a high bid and the opponent starts as low as they dare.

"Just do it!"	"No – It may not be the best solution."
	"We cannot justify spending £100k on a quick fix that might not work."
"But I need action by June."	"What do you need to see by June?"
"Some training courses competed."	"Why?"
"It is the sales conference and I promised the Board that I would arrange some more sales training."	"Let me quickly look at the problem and we will produce some evidence of sales training interventions by June, but I need your help in looking at the real problem."
"No, just organise the training."	"What do you want the training to achieve?"
"More sales: leave it to me to just organise more sales training for everyone by June."	"No, we cannot justify a quick fix for £100k."
"But it's my budget – just do it."	"I may be able to do that if you give me a week to complete the needs analysis. Otherwise I cannot support using £100k on sales training."

Some bargaining principles

In classic bargaining, people start high and low and progressively move to a compromise.

Two men haggling over a car

The buyer wants to spend £3,900; the seller wants to sell for £4,100.

Buyer	Seller
"How much?" (Never move first.)	"£4,500."
"Oh! … Now, it's not worth that much." (Try to make him move down first.)	"Well, I would accept £4,400." (Only move in small steps.)
"It is 5 years old and the price guide says £3,700 is a good price." (Low opening bid, uses first bit of information.)	"But this is in excellent condition. In my guide the top guide price is more like £4,200, and this also has a low mileage." (Plays his first bit of information.) "How much can you afford?"
"I can afford plenty but I want a fair price – how about £3,800?"	"Well, I want £4,200 and you are offering £3,800 – how about if we split the difference and agree to £4,000? After all, it is fully taxed." (Plays final bargaining chip.)

In bargaining, people tend to move to a compromise

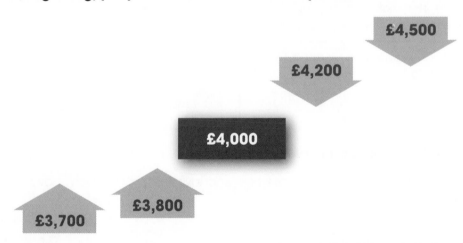

And remember to only share information one piece at a time.

The trick is to recognise when you are in a bargaining meeting. If you are, the tricks of game are:

- It is them and us.
- Work out your power versus their power.
- Have a list of bargaining points ready.
- Get them to start first.
- Only give away a little at a time.
- If you have to give something away, make sure that you win a concession from them.
- Have a final bargaining chip ready (to throw in to close the deal).

If you are having "problems" with a "difficult" client, you need to decide:

- Have you really understood their view of the world?
- Have you built sufficient rapport and trust?
- Is joint problem-solving working?
- Are they using power?
- Are you in a bargaining meeting?
- If so, what power do you have?
- Switch to a bargaining strategy.

Calculate your power versus their power and their likely bargaining ploys.

An example from real experience: Interaction between the client and their business partner (who represents IT).

The clients starts by aiming to de-power the internal consultant, even before the meeting starts:

- You are too expensive;
- IT never deliver;
- So-and-so will get that done quicker;
- It's your fault;

- We know more about it than you do;
- We are not sure what value you add;
- I haven't chosen …

This is softening up the business partner.

The opening bid is:

- Do everything I ask!

In the back of their minds, the business partner is also undermined by the negative messages from their own senior management:

- We have to deliver to prove our worth;
- We need to deliver some quick wins then we can earn the right to be involved in more strategic projects;
- We have to do the best we can in the situation;
- We need the money.

So the business partner goes into the needs analysis meeting on the back foot and "talks themselves" into being an "order taker" rather than valued partner/consultant.

- I need to do what they want.

To cope with this negative self-talk, clever business partners may talk themselves into success and build up their bargaining position.

Our strengths are:

- Our engagement skills;
- We have a consulting process;
- We are experienced – we know about the projects that have not worked and what would make them work.

Our power is:

- Working with us, they are more likely to be successful;
- We cost less than external resources;
- They have no external spend;
- We own the technical governance;
- We grant access to the designers and developers;
- We have the IT partner to support us;
- We can say no.

Our tactics are:

- Be open about previous failures;
- Be assertive about our experience and competence;
- Aim for joint problem solving;
- "We all work for the same company";
- Focus on our shared goal;
- We share same results/bonuses.

Our walk away position is:

- If we cannot prove the cost of the performance gap;
- We cannot sanction technical investment in a solution
- We say no and escalate it to our boss.

Summary

At the start of the meeting you are gaining entry and building your credibility.

Watch out for game playing and the misuse of power. If the client is not being authentic then tackle this as the problem.

In most cases the client will react rationally so we can move on to the first step in the process ... *Contracting*.

Fun:

Try watching *Dragon's Den* on TV for a good example of bargaining behaviour.

A8 Contracting and defining the problem

Even with very supportive clients we are still in the first phase – **BUILDING TRUST AND RAPPORT**. You have not yet earned the right to challenge the client, so your questions need to be neutral and non-threatening.

In the simple version of the 7-step process, step 1 is called: "What is the problem?". Actually, this can be misleading. You just need the client's first view of what doctors would call the **presenting** problem at this stage. It is most important not to define the real problem but to leave things fairly fluid at the start of the meeting.

The initial questions need to be very low key and non-threatening. The first step in influencing is to listen to your client. By listening and asking open questions the clients will open up about their problem and think that you are interested. The result will be that you will start to build some respect and credibility, and you will gain information about the client.

We start the meeting by matching our tone of voice and level of enthusiasm to the client's, perhaps repeating the initial presenting problem back to the client. It is important to go with the energy that the client is displaying. If they are enthusiastic, be enthusiastic. If they mention a pet solution, go with that solution – repeat their words back to them, for example:

> *"We need a CRM package."*
> Repeat:*" So you want a CRM package?"*

Write down the problem statement as "want a CRM package".

At this very early stage it is most important to go along with the energy of the client and be perceived as someone helpful.

Continue to be helpful and respectful and match their energy as you complete the contracting:

> *"How long have you got for this meeting?"*

and

> *"What you expect to get from that time?"*

In this way you are gradually moving the client away from the emotional attachment to this solution by matching their energy and offering no challenge or pushback. You slowly move to a more rational/adult approach by asking permission to do so with a closed question to which it is very difficult to say "No":

"Is it okay if I ask a few questions?"

Then make sure that you have a clear contract for the meeting by summarising and testing understanding, and use another closed question to get you started, for example:

"So we will finish by 12.00. You want to have achieved x by then? I want to use a problem analysis process to look at where we are now and where you want to get to – is that okay?"

Once you have got this far you can start to draw out a rich picture of the system that performs by asking another non-threatening question:

"Who is involved?"

In this way the first two steps can be used to manage the emotional part of the meeting; get into rapport with the client; and manage their expectations.

A9 **Drawing the System Diagram**

In the initial workshops we call this mapping out **who is involved**. What we are actually doing is drawing a simple system diagram or map of the client's view of their problems.

Mapping the client's business

This does not mean learning everything about their business, but working with them to map out the system they work within. You can do some of this before you meet the client, for example:

- Find their organisation chart and ask them to update it;
- Work with their more junior managers or your colleagues to map out the system that they work within;
- Create a map of their systems and processes.
- Do as much as you can with a new client to show that you have done your homework.

Then, work with them to validate and add their view of their business environment. For example, I worked with the senior managers of a UK bank to map out what their HR system looked like.

I asked the naïve questions:

- "Who are your customers?"
- "What do they want from you?"
- "When a request comes in who deals with it?"
- "Where does it go next?"
- "Where next?"
- "How does the solution get delivered?"
- "Who by?"

We ended up with diagram a bit like this, but much more complex with times, forms, system names and numbers of people included:

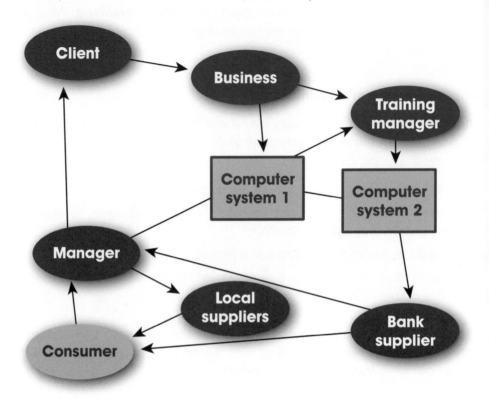

Just by doing this, the client started to reflect on the problem:

- "Yes, it is too complicated."
- "I can see that it is easier for local managers to go to local suppliers."

The managers had lived with system and the complaints for years but had never drawn a diagram to represent it.

As one of my follow-up workshop participants put it:

> *"One of the most important things is looking at who is involved. (Even though we have been involved for four years.)"*

Drawing diagrams like this with your clients can help solve problems and prove that you really understand the client's environment.

The Economic and Social Research Council (ESRC) study also showed

"Consultants needed to have a thorough grasp of the business, both from their own experience and from insightful questioning. Frustrations arose when consultants failed to appreciate the uniqueness of a client's circumstances and seemingly imposed standard, untailored solutions."

Drawing the system diagram is a key part of building trust and rapport. By sitting side-by-side with the client and mapping our their view of the world you are:

- Actively listening;
- Showing that you understand the uniqueness of their situation;
- Creating a shared picture to manage the rest of the process.

If you have first built sufficient rapport, you will then be better able to make the client face up to their real problems by asking some challenging questions.

The key questions to answer before we move on to the next phase are:

"Have we got a good enough picture of the people involved to move on?"

"Have we built enough rapport and trust to start to investigate the real problems?"

A10 **What is active listening?**

The most important partnering skills are the abilities to:

- Listen;
- Hear what has been said;
- Recognise important words and phrases;
- Write down what has been said.

As these are skills they need practice and feedback in order to improve. Ideally, ask a colleague or your coach to listen to you in a client meeting and record your use of the following consulting behaviours:

Attending	mirroring and matching body language and tone of voice, keeping comfortable eye contact
Short encouragers	e.g. "aha" and "mm" to acknowledge that information has been understood without interrupting
Using the client's words	repeating back exactly what the client said – writing down the client's key words
Seeking information	asking open questions e.g. "what", "who", "when" and "how" to get the client to expand
Reflecting feeling	catching explicitly expressed or inferred emotion e.g. you said "That is the problem."
Summarising	"So where you are now is …?"
Testing understanding	"So let me just check …"
Persistent open questions	to get below the surface meaning to deeper meaning
Discriminating	recognising and repeating key words, deeper meaning and distress cues

On the other hand the following are poor consulting behaviours:

- Closed questions;
- Leading questions;
- Multiple questions;
- Accepting everything the client says;
- Writing down long sentences;
- Giving information;
- Jumping to solutions;
- Making suggestions;
- Taking over – what I would do is …

Summary of building trust and rapport

- Before you meet the client do what you can to build your credibility.

- Are you aware of yourself? (Use tools like Myers Briggs to increase your self awareness.)

- Are you aware of the client's preferences?

- When you meet the clients, spend time building rapport.

- What out for game playing and manipulation.

- Trust your feelings, state your approach, behave in an "Adult" way and see if your client reacts in an Adult way.

- If not, you may be in a power negotiation, where you need to calculate your power position versus your client's.

- Depending on your power position, decide whether to challenge, acquiesce or walk away - if you are not sure, walk away.

- If you have built trust and rapport then write down the presenting problem (do not challenge at this point).

- Start the task part of the meeting by drawing out a non-threatening system diagram of who is involved in the problem.

- Concentrate on active listening throughout the "building trust and rapport" phase.

Contents

4B Facing up to the problem

In this phase, we need to be much more challenging because we will **quantify the performance gap**.

The key consulting behaviours are:

- asking a lot of short, open questions;
- challenging;
- quantifying the current state;
- contrasting with the desired state;
- quantifying the gap.

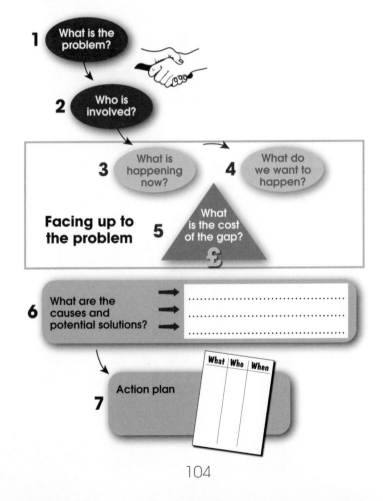

B1 Words and meaning

In my previous book I suggested that you might need to ask five open questions to get to something measurable when you are investigating the current state:

What

Who

Why

When

and **How**

How do we use these open questions?

Essentially we ask open questions to help the client to understand their own words and to realise where they are now versus where they want to be. I know this sounds a bit odd but the words we use often do not specifically say what we mean.

What do people mean by the words they use? Try this example – what do you think of when I say:

"The car is on the driveway."

What was your image?

- Mine was of an old station wagon in an American white picket fenced suburb (because we have just had an American friend to stay).
- My friend thought of his Porsche on his drive in Manchester.
- My other friend thought of her people carrier (which she hates).

You will have had your own image and it is just the same in business. When a client says the team is "ineffective", what does that mean?

As consultants we need to help the client reveal a deeper level of understanding so that we can gain a common understanding, giving us a measure against which we can quantify the performance gap.

B2   Deep and surface structure meaning

Neuro Linguistic Programming (NLP) has a very useful concept of surface and deep structure of language. The theory goes something like this:

The world contains too much information for our brains to take in, therefore we only select some of the millions of bits of information available. This is **DELETION**.

And from this we create a simplified version. This is **DISTORTION**.

And then we **GENERALISE**

so that what we say is a simplification of what we actually mean.

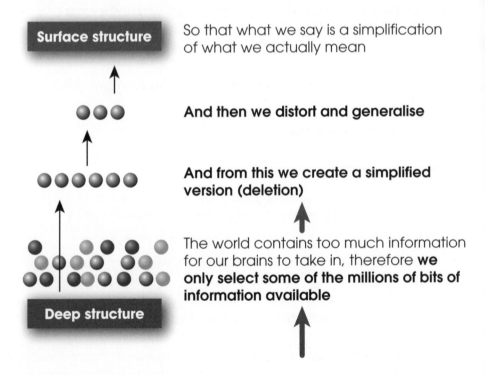

Surface structure	So that what we say is a simplification of what we actually mean
●●●	**And then we distort and generalise**
●●●●●●	**And from this we create a simplified version (deletion)**
	The world contains too much information for our brains to take in, therefore **we only select some of the millions of bits of information available**
Deep structure	

And to move from "deep structure" to "surface structure", we generalise, change and leave out parts of our ideas when we speak to others.

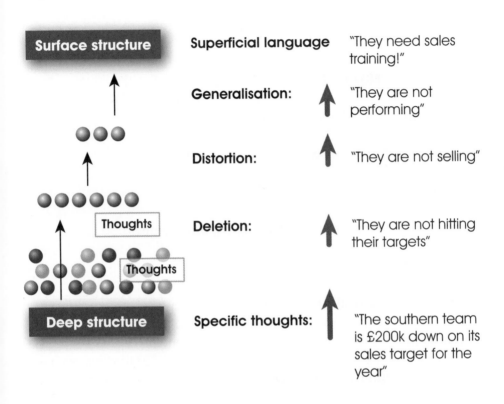

Surface structure	**Superficial language**	"They need sales training!"
	Generalisation:	"They are not performing"
	Distortion:	"They are not selling"
	Deletion:	"They are not hitting their targets"
Deep structure	**Specific thoughts:**	"The southern team is £200k down on its sales target for the year"

In step-3 of the process, when the client is discussing their current state they are often anxious and defensive. This results in surface language, for example:

Consultant: "How are things going at the moment?"
(Open question)

Client: "**Not bad**."

Consultant: "Oh, what does "not bad" mean?"

Client: "Well, **not as good as we could be**."

Consultant: "What could it be?"

Client: "Well, we **could be hitting our targets**."

Consultant: "What are your targets?"

Client: "**£3 million**."

Consultant: "And how are you doing at the moment?"

Client: "**Just a bit below**."

Consultant: How much are you missing by?

Client: "**£200,000**."

Consultant: "So you are hitting £2.8 million at the moment?"

Client: "**Yes**, that was this year's performance."

Notice in this case that the consultant has continued probing to a deeper level until they find something quantifiable.

The simplest way to think about how we use language is to watch out for **deletions, distortions** and **generalisations** and ask a **what, why, who** or **when question** to dig a little deeper.

In NLP, they go further with categorising some of our linguistic tactics. Here are some examples of questions to move people to a deeper level:

Tactic	Surface language	Questions
Deletion and unspecified noun	That system was built.	Who built the system?
Deletion	They are not telling us what is going wrong.	Who is not telling us?
Unspecified verb	He travelled to Manchester.	How did he travel?
Nominalizations When a verb has been turned into a noun	If the training had been done properly …	Who is training who and how?
Pre-suppositions	When you are experienced you will know.(Implies that you lack experience.)	What will I know?
Generalisations	I can't change.	What would happen if you did?
Necessity	You must rinse it!	What would happen if you didn't?
Judgements	It is the best system for us!	Who is telling us?
Comparisons	4-4-2 is a better defensive formation.	Than what?
Complex links	I can see from your frown that this is too complex for you.	How does that mean that?

B3 Aggressive questions!

I hope you can see that the questioning in the right hand column of the table above could appear very aggressive.

In everyday life we make generalisations and bend meanings, as well as leaving things out. Most of the time this is fine but sometimes it can disguise and hide the real issues that the client needs to face.

You have to be very careful in probing around the performance gap.

> It's not the questions you use but **how** you use them that is important.

But **beware that you need to build up a high level of trust before you can challenge and question like this**. NLP calls the making sense of words the "Meta Model". In *Introducing NLP* by O'Connor and Seymour they describe:

> *Roberts Dilts tells how he was in a linguistics class at the University of Santa Cruz in the early 1970's when John Grinder taught the Meta Model in one two-hour period. It was on a Thursday when he turned the class loose on the Meta Model. The following Tuesday half the class came in looking extremely dejected. They had alienated their lovers, their teachers and their friends, cutting them to pieces with the Meta Model. Rapport is the first step in any NLP pattern.*

It is the same in performance consulting. All that hard work in listening and building trust and rapport in steps 1 and 2 can be undone by too aggressive questioning in steps 3, 4 and 5. On the other hand, you also need to challenge the client to help them see their own problems and to enable them move from their surface description of problems to a deeper level.

B4 **Distress cues**

On a recent workshop, someone asked me what to watch out for in the client's non-verbal and verbal reactions. The most obvious things I watch for are sign of distress:

* nervous giggling and laughter;
* leaning back and making a sucking noise;
* banging the pen on the table and saying "That's the real problem!"
* grimacing;
* frowning;
* Speaking in a aised voice, e.g. "They should be doing it!"
* Parental words like "should", "ought" and "must".

If you spot one of these signs, go for it, but gently:

Ask in a calm, soft voice:

* "Oh, why should they be doing it?"

Or just repeat their words and perhaps imitate their tone:

* "You said "They **should** be doing it!""

By acting as a mirror to the client you can often learn a lot about their own problems by hearing their own words repeated.

B5 Bouncing between negative and positive

In steps 3, 4 and 5 we are helping the client see and face up to their problem.

In this phase it helps to have the contrast between the existing state and the desired state.

I usually use two columns on an A3 piece of paper.

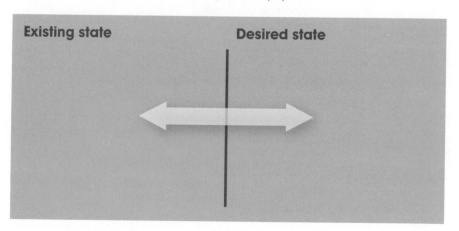

Use you own headings.

It may be quicker to use:

As Is – To Be
Now – Want
Pain – Gain

Whatever works for you!

The point is to help the client see a contrast – the difference or gap between where they are and where they want to move to.

The process goes something like this:

Existing performance	Desired performance
Consultant: So what are they doing at the moment?	
Client: It is an ineffective team.	
Oh? …what do you mean by ineffective?	
They should be monitoring the work much closer.	
Which work?	
Outgoing proposals.	
What is wrong with outgoing proposals?	
They have too many errors in them.	
Oh.. how many?	
We have failed to answer critical questions.	
What is the implication of that?	
We have only won 24% of the contracts we bid for this year and lost 2 contracts by failing to answer the questions in the "Invitation to Tender" properly.	
How much were those contracts worth?	
£500,000.	What do you want this team to be achieving?
	We need to win 40% of the contacts we bid for.
	And how many times would it be okay to fail to answer the tender questions correctly?
	None.
	Can you describe what you really want this team to be doing?
	Yes. Working thoroughly – checking all tender requirements against our submission and winning 40% of the bids we put in.
	What would that be worth to you?
	Winning 40% is worth about a £million to us and, as I said, those two orders lost through errors were worth £500K.

So can we say that this gap is worth at least £500k and probably £1 million?

YES!

Is it worth doing something about?

Absolutely!

Why is it worth doing something about?

Well, it's worth a lot of money.

What does that mean to you personally?

Well, apart from my bonus, it's the pride in doing a good job and a chance to beat department Y ...

Good, let's move on to investigating why this team has this gap because, if we can find out what is stopping them, we can identify the solutions that will help.

Tip: Watch out for gaps that are too big and do not really mean anything to the client. Try to bring it down to something personal to them.

B6 The typical way that the meeting goes when you are in the "quantifying the gap" phase

Notice the large number of probing questions to drill down to something measurable.

Then you flip the negative image over to what they want to see and help your client to imagine what success looks like.

The cost of the gap is the difference between the two. Some clients will prefer to start with describing where they want to get to, whilst others will be happier with where they want to move away from: it does not matter, you can start from whichever side of the problem the client chooses.

You can start from whichever side of the paper you prefer. Some clients may be happier starting with describing where they want to get to – others will not. It does not matter where you start.

The key thing is that you need to have built up the trust and rapport so that your detailed questioning is perceived and felt as being helpful, not just challenging.

I once suffered a potential client using this "chunking down" technique on me in an interview. I felt uncomfortable and manipulated and turned down the offer of work. He had not taken the time to build rapport with me and I saw his constant questioning as aggressive rather than helpful.

So be careful:

- Build rapport first;
- Ask your questions gently;
- Watch your client's reactions;
- Give them space and time to answer.

On the other hand, what our clients value the most is this challenge:

"You helped me to see it differently."

"I hadn't thought about it like that."

"The challenge really helped me."

This is the consulting tightrope that you walk:

- Do not challenge enough and you do not add enough value;
- Challenge too much and you lose trust and rapport.

Summary

In the middle phase we help the client to **face up to their problems**.

The way to do this is to ask open questions and reflect back what you hear to the clients:

- to help reveal the surface structure of the problem;
- to uncover the deeper, more measurable, current state versus the desired state;
- and, hence, quantify the cost of the gap.

This level of questioning and challenge can only work if you have built enough **trust and rapport** with the client and your questions are perceived as being helpful.

The key question to be answered before we move on from this phase is:

"Is this gap worth doing something about?"
"What is it worth to you personally?"

If the problem is not explicit, so that you can see "deep level information" (usually numbers) about the current and future state, and client is not convinced that it is worth doing something about, then there is no point in moving on to investment in solutions!

After all, we wouldn't know how much it was worth investing or what success would look like, even if we reached it!

Building powerful solutions

Contents

4C **Building powerful solutions**

This phase is much more comfortable for you and the client. It is characterised by:

- pulling things together;
- making things concrete;
- commitment to action;
- closed questions, e.g. "So we have agreed to X?";
- agreeing the action plan.

Enjoy this phase. It is also your chance to bring in your expertise and make suggestions, secure in the knowledge that they are appropriate because you know what the problem is.

It is human to make sense of patterns, to join up the dots and make patterns (Gestalt psychology). We are more comfortable with the concrete and most clients jump too quickly to the comfort of solutions and action.

A simple way to structure your ideas is to think through the main possible causes for the performance gap.

The ideas generator is a series of prompts to investigate the reason for any performance gap.

The Ideas Generator

Step 6 – What are the causes and potential solutions?

Try to generate as many solutions as possible. Suspend judgement as to their feasibility, and write them all down.

What do the key players lack?

Knowledge or skill	Idea
Do they lack some knowledge?	Give them the knowledge (just tell them)?
Do they lack some knowledge and skill?	Make the performance easier in some way by: • Simplifying the tasks? • Splitting the job? • Designing checklists? • Clarifying performance standards?
Were they once able to do it?	Try practice, better information and feedback.
Have they got the capability to learn how to do this?	Consider training them and providing learning materials.
If they haven't got the capability...	Can we transfer them to a job that they can do or terminate their employment?

Motivation

Do they get feedback on performance?	Provide clear goals and regular feedback on positive as well as negative performance.
If they do it right, do they suffer in any way, e.g. by being given more work?	Reduce the punishment for high performance. Introduce rewards and incentives.
Are they being rewarded for low performance?	Stop the rewards.
Do people lack self-esteem?	Help them visualise success, set positive goals. Catch people doing things right, build on success.

Environment

Is there anything wrong with their environment, methods, equipment?	Improve.
Are the managers helping?	Improve management.
Any other obstacles?	Try to remove them.

C2 **How do we find the correct solutions?**

It is very simple. We do not need to strive to invent solutions, as once we identify the causes of the gap, the solutions will be the antidotes, e.g. if the cause is lack of knowledge, then the solution is to give them knowledge, and so on.

Example

I was once asked to design a leadership programme for supervisors in a mail sorting office. When I asked the client about this, they said things like: "they lack fire in their belly"; "people never get back from breaks on time"; "they don't have control over the staff".

When I talked to some supervisors I found that:

- They had all been promoted from small offices into this large sorting office;
- They were promoted on seniority and time in the job;
- They had had no training in how to be a supervisor – it was assumed that because they had been promoted they could do the job;
- The sorting office was on four floors and covered a large area;
- The teams were highly unionised and had been doing the tasks for a long time;
- The supervisors had an office in the corner of one level and no mobile phones;
- The sorting equipment was causing breakage and fixing it took staff resources from the main team;
- They had no clear objectives.

No wonder they were not reaching their targets! We did not do any leadership training; instead the managers concentrated on solutions to the above.

C3 How to turn an idea into action

It may be enough to enthuse your client with the logic of your joint solutions, after all you have:

- Listened to them;
- Shown that you understand the complexities of their situation through a jointly drawn system diagram;
- Shown that you can see the world as they see it;
- Helped them to see what success will look like in the desired performance;
- Helped them to feel the pain of their current state, confirming that they want to move away from it;
- Quantified the cost of doing nothing – which is a cost that they can compare with the investment in any solutions.

You have also worked with them systematically to identify the most likely causes for the performance gap and they have chosen the most cost-effective solutions to try first.

So, if your client has the power, they may be able to implement your joint solutions immediately. But what happens if they have to take their case forward to others to win approval for action?

Your solutions may make wonderful sense and have financial benefits to the organisation but may never prosper in the powerful world of competing ideas and power holders within your organisation.

Action only happens if its power system chooses to allow it to happen.

Has your client got the power to see an idea through?

An idea will never make it into action unless it can compete with other ideas.

An idea needs to grow in substance. This usually involves engaging a power supply to input energy into the idea, enough for it to compete successfully and gain more resources than other ideas.

Has your client got enough power:

- To input energy into this idea?
- To grow it until it is big enough to survive and prosper?
- To win resources for it?
- To "sell" it to others?
- And to allow it to compete successfully with other ideas?

Action only happens if the people involved feel that they have a choice and have chosen to take action.

C4 **Drawing stakeholder maps**

You may already have done this in your system diagram, but if not it is important to do it now. It will enable you to help the client to think through who needs to be engaged to support your solutions to move to action.

For example, who has expectations of a business partner?

What are these expectations?

Directors	Unlimited free training, HR and IT to help them achieve their business objectives.
Senior managers and the CEO	Business partner to be a free pair of hands, a proven link to business performance improvement.
HR Director	Reduce cost and meet our obligations, deliver the promised solutions on time
Training, HR and IT managers	Clear and realistic specification for projects.

I know that this is simplistic but there is a serious point.

People often have expectations that conflict and, so, cannot all be met. It is better to get these out in the open and tackle them. Working hard is not the answer.

As an internal consultant you can literally position yourself on the diagram and show how you contribute to helping the client meet their expectations. In addition, you can use it to explain the expectations you have of your other stakeholders, so it can be a useful way in to explaining and contracting about your role. Drawing a map of the people involved can also involve drawing a stakeholder map.

Try drawing your stakeholder map now

What expectations do your stakeholders have of you?

How will you meet these?

Some key roles to identify are:

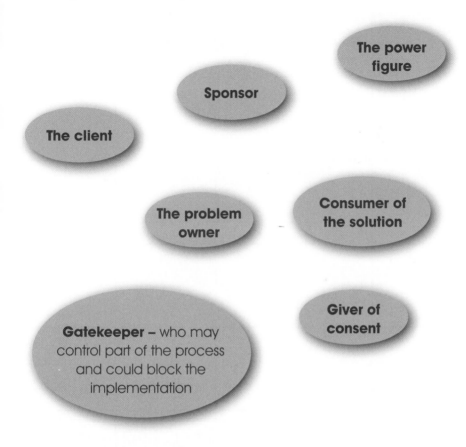

What sort of power do they have?

- Position power?
- Control of resources?
- Network power?
- Expert power?

Think about each stakeholder

Stakeholder	What will inhibit them from supporting this idea?	What will help them?	What do you need to do?
The client			
The sponsor			
The power figure			
Problem owner			
Consumers			
Consent givers			
Gatekeepers			

Summary of 4C Building Powerful Solutions

- This phase is much more comfortable for you and the client because you are moving from the fluid to the concrete.
- Use the Ideas generator to investigate possible reasons for the performance gap.
  - Do the key players lack
  - Knowledge?
  - Skills?
  - Motivation?
  - Or are Environmental factors getting in their way?

- Just because you come up with some brilliant solutions does not mean that they will be actioned – you will need to work with your client to engage a power supply to invest energy into the idea.
- Draw a stakeholder map and work out what will inhibit the stakeholders from supporting the idea and what will help them to support it.

Thinking about the process in a new way

The 7-step process can be thought of as three distinct phases.

A. Building trust and rapport

B. Facing up to the problem

C. Building powerful solutions

Consulting is not a game of perfect, it does not matter whether or not you follow the 7-steps, as long as you help the client face up to their problems.

Each of the following involves different consulting behaviours

A. Listening and building rapport

B. Challenge and questioning to get below the superficial language.

C. Consecutive ideas to move forward.

Watch out for clients misusing their power and playing games.

The best defence you have is to stay in an adult frame of mind.

The key skills you need are to listen, hear what has been said, recognise key words, repeat them and write them down.

Pulling it all together

Can you recognise the use of the 7-step process and business partnering skills in the following examples?

Business partner, Brian 1, starts his new role

Brian 1, the business partner, recently joined Roberts Music from his previous job as a Training Director for Roberts Biscuits, a small subsidiary. He was offered some training in business partner skills but turned it down because he felt that he already had the experience needed to do the role. In the first week in the role Brian encountered 3 key clients with separate requests.

1. Colin, the Chief Executive, called him in

Colin: "Hi, Brian, good to have you on board. I have just a few minutes before the board meeting. Last year we all agreed that we needed more leaders in the company – I am sure you will agree. Now that you are on board I want you to arrange it as a priority. I want to see some leadership training happening this year. Sorry, got to go to the board meeting".

2. Sonia, the sales director, arranged a meeting

Sonia: "Good to meet you Brian, how is your first day going? I just want to talk to you about some creativity training. 'Global' used this guy, Greg Magic. He is an ex-magician, did a great job I hear. Please can you arrange some sessions for the sales team? I want to keep the sessions short, half-day ones should do. Can you cover it on the training budget? I want to do something by September."

3. Fred, the marketing director, comes to see Brian

Fred: "Hello Brian, I believe that you are our new business partner, and that we have to go through you for IT projects. I attended the International Sales Conference in Geneva last week. Most of our competitors are using integrated CRM software. Please ask IT to contact me about implementing integrated CRM urgently this year across the company."

How does Brian react?

At the end of his first week, he is pretty pleased with himself:

1. He has found out from Colin's PA that Colin wants the top 200 managers to go through leadership training. Brian has researched 3 business schools and chosen Pratfield for a 9-day programme for all the managers. He is most proud of the fact that has negotiated the price down from £1,800 per person to £1,500. Colin's PA says that Colin is delighted.

2. He has checked out Greg Magic, who seems like a good guy. He checked his references and attended an exciting, open version of his one-day creativity workshop. Greg has tailored the workshop to meet Robert's needs, i.e. 3 early-evening sessions, spread over 3 weeks. Sonia is delighted.

3. He made friends with Alex, the IT Director, and arranged a meeting with Fred. He did not see the need to attend, as it was an IT solution. Later Alex told him that they were implementing a company-wide CRM system next year at a cost of £1.3 million.

On Friday night Brian decided to celebrate with a good bottle of wine – it had been a good first week.

Nine months later …

The company is in trouble. Colin calls an emergency board meeting to tackle the problems of: losing Sonia to a competitor; a recent newspaper article declaring that Roberts's music catalogue is looking out-of-date; and sales being down by 25%. In an emergency round of cutting non-value-adding staff, Brian is made redundant.

How could it have gone?

Business partner, Brian 2, starts his new role

Brian 2, the business partner, recently joined Roberts from his previous job as a Training Director for a small subsidiary. He attended a workshop on business partner skills and made sure that it was the common process used by all internal consultants throughout Roberts Music. In the first week in the role Brian encountered three key clients with separate requests.

1. Colin, the Chief Executive, called him in

Colin: "Hi, Brian, good to have you on board. I have just a few minutes before the board meeting. Last year we all agreed that we needed more leaders in the company – I am sure you will agree. Now that you are on board I want you to arrange it as a priority. I want to see some leadership training happening this year. Sorry, got to go to the board meeting".

Brian 2: "Very exciting Colin, we did something very similar at Biscuits. It takes a bit of thinking to make sure we get the best out of that sort of investment. When have you got time to discuss it so that I can be crystal clear that it will do what you want? Don't worry about it now, I will book a meeting with your PA. Have a good board meeting."

Later in the week, Brian 2 is in a scheduled 1 hour meeting with Colin:

Brian 2: "How was the board meeting? … I think you know Margaret Brown at Biscuits? I helped her with the merger …I see that you support United. I have a season ticket too – it should be a good season …"

"How long have you got now? … Good, 40 minutes should do it … I want to make sure that this leadership solution really adds value to the organisation … Is it okay if I ask you some questions? Good!"

"Let's start with who you want it for. Your PA gave me your organisation chart. I see that you have 200 line managers reporting to you. Who are the key people involved in leading your part of the business?"

"All of them?"

"Who would be the priority?"

"I see, your 15 direct reports who run the business areas."

"Please could you highlight the individuals on the diagram – here is a pen – do you mind if we sit over here so I can see the diagram?"

"Of the 15 business areas, which are you most concerned about?"

"Yes, I see that music sales across the company are a critical issue at the moment and the 8 area sales managers are key people in achieving sales.

"So, is it all 8?"

"And Sonia, the sales director …Why is that?"

"You are worried that she might leave?"

"And there is no immediate successor in line."

"What effect would losing Sonia have on your sales?"

"So it would set you back up to 6 months whilst you recruited from outside. Wow – how much could that be worth?"

"So, about £300k lost sales impetus and £30k headhunting cost?"

"There is no development for Sonia or the area marketing managers?"

"How are sales going this year?"

"Sales are 15% down this year?"

"How much is that worth?"

"So, the gap is worth £1 million."

"You want a leadership course to give your 8 key players some development to encourage them to stay and to give them some skills to tackle the sales gap?"

"Let's imagine that they were performing as you really wanted — what would you see?"

"Let me repeat that."

"Sonia, happy in her role and discussing a 3-year strategy with you, and you confident that she will see it through. Additionally you would like us to have 2 possible successors who could take over from her."

"And the area managers are hitting their sales targets?"

"Do any of them hit their targets at the moment?"

"So Robin is the only area manager above target?"

"What does he do differently?"

"Shall I go and see him to find out exactly what works in his area?"

"Please can you make an introduction?"

"Is there an opportunity for me to report back on my findings?"

"So, to you and Sonia in your monthly sales meeting with her, okay".

"Let me summarise where we are. We have 3 main issues:

1. There is no successor to Sonia and she is a key player.

2. You do not have a 3 year strategy and are not confident that she will stay.

3. Sales are down by 15%, which could be a gap of £1 million if we do nothing about it.

We have 15 minutes left, which one do you want to investigate first?"

"Okay, the sales gap is the most important."

"We have already agreed that I will interview Robin — please make the introduction for me. Also, book me into your monthly meeting with Sonia. We will look at what works for Robin and see if we can spread the best practice around the others."

"I will make the sales issue my priority."

The lack of a 3-year sales strategy – have you told Sonia that you want one?"

"Does she know how to develop one?"

"Has she got the skills to do it?"

"Is she motivated – Ah, I can see that the current sales gap could prevent her from looking ahead."

"Any environmental factors? Oh, so her review is imminent."

"So, what are you going to do?"

"Raise your concerns at her review."

"Give her a 3-year bonus deal."

"I will work with you and her on the sales gap problem."

"How about if we use this performance gap analysis process together?"

"I will facilitate a meeting between the 3 of us."

"If you can set it up in Sonia's review …"

"We will need 2-3 hours to be on the safe side."

"Okay."

Now, let's tackle 'no successor for Sonia'."

Well, the action we have agreed will help.

"Let's re-visit this problem after meeting Sonia and tackling the urgent sales gap."

"Perhaps you could just keep the need for a successor in mind, and see if you can identify 2 potential successors."

"Is that okay?"

"Well, that's 40 minutes."

"We have a clear action plan."

"We have not arranged any leadership training, is that okay?"

"Did you get value out of this meeting?"

"What did I do that helped?"

"Good, let's book a regular monthly meeting."

Brian 2 walks out of the meeting and meets

Sonia, the Sales Director

Sonia: "Good to meet you Brian, how is your first day going? I just want to talk to you about some creativity training. 'Global' used this guy, Greg Magic. He is an ex-magician, did a great job I hear. Please can you arrange some sessions for the sales team? I want to keep the sessions short, half-day ones should do. Can you cover it on the training budget? I want to do something by September."

Brian 2 deals with Sonia:

"Hi, Sonia, good to meet you. I have just been in with Colin. Yes, creativity sounds very interesting. We will have more time to talk soon, but one quick question: When we have done this creativity training for your team, what sort of things do you want to start seeing?"

"So you want a fresher approach."

"More new music in the catalogue?"

"Let's discuss this next week at the meeting with Colin."

Brian 2 handles Fred the Marketing director

Fred: "Hello Brian, I believe that you are our new business partner, and that we have to go through you for IT projects. I attended the International Sales Conference in Geneva last week. Most of our competitors are using integrated CRM software. Please ask IT to contact me about implementing integrated CRM urgently this year across the company."

This is how Brian 2 responds:

"Hi, Fred. Good to meet you. I think you know Dave in Distribution? We play tennis together."

"I just need to ask you a few business partner questions to clarify your business needs before we get together with IT. Is that okay?"

"Who do you want the integrated CRM software for?"

"I see."

"How are they performing at the moment?"

"So, they are 15% below target. How much is that worth?

"Wow, so this is a £1 million problem!"

"So, if you had an integrated system, what would that allow you to do?"

"You could make sure that the sales people spent 80% of their time with the 20% who are key clients?"

"How much of their time do they spend with key clients at the moment?"

"I see you do not know – what do you think it is?"

"I see – 20:80 rather than 80:20."

"If you reversed the figure, do you think giving more attention to the key clients could close the sales gap?"

"So, again, this is a £1million problem?"

"Who is the key person accountable for making sure the sales people spend 80% of their time on the key clients?"

"The sales managers."

"Do they know how to do this?"

"So, they do not have the data."

"That's why you want an integrated CRM system?"

"Well, I guess a new CRM system could take months to implement – is there any quicker way we could find out their sales activity?"

"Can we implement that immediately?"

"Good."

"When they have the data, do they have the skills to sell to key clients?"

"Probably?"

"Are they motivated?"

"I see, they feel more comfortable with the small music stores. I wonder if we have the right sales people?"

"Well, let's start with the data and work with the sales managers to explain what to do with more time with the larger clients."

"Have you anyone who is already good at this?"

"Shall we talk to Sonia to identify if there is anyone? Then I will interview them and find out what they do."

"Good."

"If you sort out the short term sales activity data, I will meet Sonia and find a high performer to interview. Perhaps we can have a joint meeting with Sonia to see if we can feedback the data and best practice ideas to the key sales managers?"

"When we get over this sales gap, we will look at a longer term solution and an integrated CRM system. Is that okay?"

"Good."

Brian 2 finishes his first week with a good idea of the urgent business issues and confident that he is working with the management team as a respected business partner.

Nine months later …

The company has achieved its sales targets. Brian 2 is a regular member of the board meeting. He reports on his evaluation of his first 3 projects as a business partner for the company. He estimates the value he adds as a saving of £1.6 million of inappropriate training; and a contribution towards closing the £1 million sales gap. He is given a pay rise and asked to move on to the board permanently.

He is acting as a **true business partner**.

The End

Well, that's all folks!

I have tried to explain how to be a successful business partner and performance consultant. You need a process and some consulting skills, but you also need to tackle your own self-awareness and cope with the irrational world of organisational solutioneering. If you can stay true and ask open questions with integrity and follow a gap analysis process, you can do enormous good in the organisation. The internal consultants I work with have stopped many millions of pounds of wasted investment and they usually win extra resources for fewer interventions but with a proven business value. Good luck!

If you would like some help with your performance problems, contact me on nigel@performconsult.co.uk

Nigel Harrison
Performance Consulting – UK
www.performconsult.co.uk

Bibliography

What I would recommend first:

Berne, E. (1964) *Games People Play* (Penguin Books)

Carnegie, D. (1964) *How to Win Friends and Influence People* (Simon & Schuster).

Carter Ruth, Martin, John, Mayblin Bill, Munday Michael (1984) *Systems, Management and Change* (Buckingham: Open University).

Harrison, N. (2000) *Improving Employee Performance* (Kogan Page)

O'Connor, J. and Seymour, J. (1990) *Introducing NLP* (Mandala)

Reivich, K. and Shatte, A. (2002) *The Resilience Factor – 7 Keys to Finding your Inner Strengths and Overcoming Life's Hurdles* (Broadway Books)

www.adaptive.com for a free 60 question resilience inventory

More in-depth stuff:

Block, P. (1981) *Flawless Consulting* (Pfeiffer and Co).

Charvet, S.R. (1997) *The Words that Change Minds* (Kendall/Hunt Publishing).

Gilbert, T.F (1978) *Human Competence: Engineering Worthy Performance* (McGraw Hill).

Mager, R.F. and Pipe, P. (1970) *Analysing Performance Problems* (Belmont, CA: Fearon Pitman Publishers).

Rackham, N. and Carlisle, J. (1978) *The behaviour of successful negotiators, Journal of European Industrial Training*, 2(6), pp .6-11

Robinson, D.G. and Robinson, J.C. (1995) *Performance Consulting* (San Francisco, CA: Berret-Koehler Publishers).

Tieger, P and Barron-Tieger, B (1998) *The Art of Speed Reading People* (Little Brown).